Great Gatherings

"Gather the People"

(Joel 2:16)

Book II of the Kalmus Series

Cho Larson

Rimrock, Arizona

Published by Warner House Press of Rimrock, Arizona, USA

Copyright © 2020 Cho Larson
Cover Design and Illustration © 2020 Ian Loudon, OKAY Media
Interior Design © 2020 Warner House Press

All rights reserved. No part of this book may be used or reproduced in any manner whatsoever without written permission, except in the case of brief quotations in critical articles and reviews. For more information, contact

Warner House Press
4410 E Cayuga Lane
Rimrock, AZ 86335
USA

Published 2020
Printed in the United States of America

Unless otherwise noted, all scripture quotations are taken from HOLY BIBLE, NEW INTERNATIONAL VERSION®. Copyright © 1973, 1978, 1984 by International Bible Society. Used by permission of Zondervan Publishing House.

Scripture quotations marked ESV are from The Holy Bible, English Standard Version®, Copyright © 2001 by Crossway Bibles, a publishing ministry of Good News Publishers. Used by permission. All rights reserved.

Scripture quotations marked CSB are taken from the Christian Standard Bible®, Copyright © 2017 by Holman Bible Publishers. Used by permission. Christian Standard Bible, and CSB® are federally registered trademarks of Holman Bible Publishers.

Scripture quotations marked ISV are taken from the Holy Bible: International Standard Version® Release 2.0. Copyright © 1996-2014 by the ISV Foundation. Used by permission of Davidson Press, LLC. ALL RIGHTS RESERVED INTERNATIONALLY.

Scripture quotations marked NKJV are from the New King James Version®. Copyright © 1982 by Thomas Nelson. Used by permission. All rights reserved.

Scripture quotations marked NLT are from the Holy Bible, New Living Translation, Copyright © 1996, 2004, 2007, 2013, 2015 by Tyndale House Foundation. Used by permission of Tyndale House Publishers Inc., Carol Stream, Illinois 60188. All rights reserved.

Scripture quotations marked NRSV are from the New Revised Standard Version Bible, copyright (C) 1989 National Council of the Churches of Christ in the United Satates of America. Used by permission. All rights reserved worldwide.

26 25 24 23 22 21 20 1 2 3 4 5

ISBN: 978-1-951890-05-6

And let us consider how we may spur one another on toward love and good deeds, not giving up meeting together, as some are in the habit of doing, but encouraging one another–and all the more as you see the Day approaching.
(Hebrews 10:24–25)

Blest be the tie that binds
our hearts in Christian love;
the fellowship of kindred minds
is like to that above.

Before our Maker's throne
we pour our ardent prayers;
our fears, our hopes, our aims are one,
our comforts and our cares.

We share each other's woes,
each other's burdens bear,
and often for each other flows
the sympathizing tear.

When we asunder part,
it gives us keenest pain,
but we shall still be joined in heart,
and hope to meet again.

The glorious hope revives
our courage on the way:
in perfect friendship we shall live
in God's eternal day.

John Fawcett, 1739–1817

Table of Contents

Enter Here and Prepare to Gather...vii
Author's Note..xi

Part I: Gather the Grain, New Wine, and Oil
Chapter 1: The Great Departure...3
Chapter 2: Gathered in His Name...11
Chapter 3: In the Presence of our High Priest..................43
Chapter 4: Gather to Hear and Do...53
Chapter 5: Sanctified in Gathering..61
Chapter 6: The Fullness of Christ in Fellowship..............73
Chapter 7: Together We are the Temple of the Holy Spirit...79
Chapter 8: Pillars Upon the Rock..87
Chapter 9: Together We Stand in God's Council............93

Part II: Gather All Your Children to You
Chapter 10: It Takes a Gathering to Serve....................103
Chapter 11: Serving Before our High Priest..................111
Chapter 12: Spiritual Gifts Imparted................................119
Chapter 13: Strengthened for Victory..............................127
Chapter 14: Prepared to Serve...135

PART III: His Spirit Will Gather Them
Chapter 15: Fellowship in Gathering................................143
Chapter 16: A Bond of Love...153
Chapter 17: Gathering in Shalom.......................................159
Chapter 18: A Harmonious Chorus...................................165
Chapter 19: The Power of Prayer Gatherings................171
Chapter 20: Together We Make Up What Is Lacking......179
Chapter 21: Forgiveness in Gathering.............................185
Chapter 22: Baptism Unites us with Christ....................193
Chapter 23: The Miracle of the Lord's Table.................199
Chapter 24: Gathered to God's People............................209
Chapter 25: We Assemble to Prepare for the Great Gathering...217

Enter Here and Prepare to Gather

The New Testament has many references to "one another." This is not by chance but inspired by the Spirit of Jesus who reveals the true nature of our heavenly Father. Every chapter in this study is packed with verses that draw a beautiful picture of the power and effect of gathering together in Jesus' holy name. When we hear the words of Scripture read, taught, and proclaimed in our assemblies, God's holy words empower us to worship, serve, and minister before a holy God. Throughout this study the author uses the word "gathering" more often than "church" to avoid the notion that this is about entering a building.

The author's first book of the Kalmus series is *Great Separations*. The message is a call to be separated to Christ, and by the power of the Holy Spirit overcome our weakness to accomplish the work of the Great Commission in His power and strength. An important part of this is to separate what is holy from what is common. When we are separated to Christ, His desire is to gather us together as a hen gathers her chicks. In Jesus' own words:

Jerusalem, Jerusalem, you who kill the prophets and stone those sent to you, how often I have longed to gather your children together, as a hen gathers her chicks under her wings, and you were not willing.
(Matthew 23:37)

Great Gatherings will not help you draw a bigger crowd to fill a building or stadium. No formulas for church growth are included here. Nor will the material help build social capital. It's not a study about establishing trust within a community or about making people connections. Instead, it's about our Lord Jesus who gathers us for a good purpose—to sit at the feet of our High Priest to hear him teach us with holy words. Then, when faith is added to the hearing of God's word, we come into the presence of the Spirit of Christ, empowered to do what the Scriptures compel us to do. Our purpose is to come together to honor and glorify God, to carry out the work of the church, and care for the sheep of God's pasture. It's more than a Sunday thing. To hear and do what God has called us to do must be more than a weekly meeting with friends. When people gather because of faith in Jesus' name, it's miraculous and life changing. It's a forever kind of change that is delivered by the wielding of a sword to permeate every moment of our daily lives.

*"Do not suppose that I have come to bring peace to the earth.
I did not come to bring peace, but a sword."*
(Matthew 10:34)

Jesus' statement is the heart of this study. The sword of his mouth that separates is a large part of the message of the first two books of the Kalmus series. This separation is vital because a worship gathering is not like a community meeting or a service organization luncheon. Service clubs are for the common good, but Christian gatherings are uncommon—for an eternal good. Committee meetings aren't a good fit for Jesus' servants. Their greatest moments happen when they kneel down to prayerfully search the heart of God and rise up to act accordingly. This message is essential for the postmodern church. While our gatherings are not a spiritual cure-all, they are assemblies where we may come into the fullness of Christ.

We'll learn that the "one another" teaching of the New Testament reflects the heart of the glorified Christ who is head of His body the church. The body of Christ is not a body like Jesus took on to walk among us here on earth.[1] The church is a spiritual body with functioning parts, and it includes every soul who has been redeemed by the blood of Jesus Christ. All who are in Christ are new creations and made to function as part of the whole body—a spiritual body.

In this study, we'll learn about the body of Christ and the promise of His presence.

"For where two or three gather in my name, there am I with them."
(Matthew 18:20)

This verse teaches us that it takes more than one body part to make up the body. All of us who are called by His holy name are brought together to function within a body of believers. We are Jesus' hand extended to minister and serve one another. We are His mouthpiece to speak what He speaks. We are the living, active body of Christ, and Jesus likes to hang out where His body is functioning—where all the different parts of His body work together as one. It's like someone who says, "Where you see my hands and feet at work, that's where I will be." That's how close Jesus Christ is when we come together in His name.

Our study will start with a look at the dark side of the contemporary church and how it functions in a post-modern world. It's important to see the challenges we face as the church in our day and to repent from the heart. Then we will build on the Rock, Christ Jesus, and come to delight in the ministries of our High Priest. This certainly isn't about religious organizations, denominations, or 501(c)(3) non-profit corporations, but rather about God's people who gather together in Jesus' name. With the attitude of a servant and

---
1. John 1:29.

hearts that are prepared to forgive, our voices are joined in one accord. God's abundant blessings become ours as we join together in unity to worship.

We'll learn about the many benefits of gathering together. The studies show us how a Christian assembly affects our daily lives and our forever life. What does a get-together of believers look like? We will be inspired to learn how gathering together strengthens us, provides protection, encourages us in all that is good, restores our souls, spurs us toward love, armors us up for life's battles, and prepares us to be sent out to minister and serve. We will come to understand the joys of the ministries of spiritual gifts and the delight of fulfilling our call in Christ. The blessings and wonders of shared worship will become evident in this study. We will see that when the whole truth of the Gospel message is taught, preached, and received with gladness, Jesus' presence will be confirmed in our gatherings.

We will discover the blessings of Shalom[2] given to Christ's flock. As you dig into this study, you will see the benefit of gathering where there is forgiveness, sweet fellowship, opportunities to grow in grace and knowledge of Christ, and the miraculous power of gathering together at the Lord's Table to be partakers of His body and blood. We will also learn the value of coming together to witness the wonders of baptism in the church.

This study includes an occasional use of Hebraic names of our Lord God like Yĕhovah, and for Messiah, Yeshua HaMashiach to honor God who doesn't change and to offer a sense of the historicity of our Christian faith. We have a rich history that begins with God creating the heavens and earth. We are taught these truths starting with Abel, and on to Zechariah. These traces of our history are added to open a window to see the beauty of our historic, orthodox Christian faith, and to show that this study book leads us to stand shoulder to shoulder with the champions of our faith.[3] The goal is to express historic truth with words that refresh today's student of the word. The purpose is to enter into the fullness of Christ and His body—the church.

This study will help us to profit spiritually from God's good gifts given to the church, so we can leap forward into a life of spiritual abundance. We'll learn how gathering prepares us for the great gathering when our Lord Jesus calls us home. My hope is to express the pure joy and delight of joining together with the flock in the Good Shepherd's fold so that we may live in the glorious riches of the mystery of Christ.[4]

The studies vary in length depending on the depth necessary to bring the

---

2. Shalom means peace in Hebrew.
3. Jeremiah 6:16.
4. Colossians 1:27.

truth to light. Each lesson is followed by pertinent questions to help us examine ourselves so we can lay a solid spiritual foundation in repentance. A space is provided to write notes to help in your personal or group study sessions following the questions.

When we face up to our past failings and confess our sins, we will be ready to hear God's call to enter the joy, blessings, and power of gathering in Jesus name. This is the purpose of the *Great Gatherings* study book.

Author's Note

A pivotal moment for me as a Christian occurred when traumatic events unfolded in my local church. The chaos brought on a sense of despair and a felt need to be done with church. It was worth asking, "Who needs this kind of trouble?" My heart's cry went out to the Lord one morning as I stood at my kitchen window to look over the fields of green grass. Holstein cows grazed without concern in the fresh pasture by the river. My cry to the Lord was a plea for something besides the divisive chaos I'd experienced. The turmoil grieved me because it drove many of my friends from fellowship and tore families apart. Then, just as clear as if it was an audible voice to my ears: "To whom will you go?"

The question calmed me and taught me that there is only one church, and it will prevail. The people who make up a local church may become fractured, but the church universal will be victorious. The blessings and benefits of gathering far outweigh the difficult times. We can rise above the fray and enjoy the ministries of our High Priest in our assemblies. The troubles, challenges, and broken church moments will then seem like mere bumps in the road. Challenges will come and go, but Christ Jesus is the Rock on which the church is built. In the end we, the church, will withstand every storm.

That very day I made a life changing decision to continue to be a part of the body of Christ—the church. And today I'm so grateful for those enlightening words. Since then I've prayed earnestly for my local gathering and God's people as a whole. I constantly send up appeals for those who have been driven away from the church. What is written here is an expression of those prayers. This study book is written prayerfully and is presented before the Lord Almighty as a petition for God's people—the sheep of His pasture.

When this project began, I had a little understanding of the benefits and power of gathering in Jesus' name. As I researched, studied, listened, and wrote, it's as if fallow ground was prepared and seeded to blossom and become a beautiful landscape. I'm blessed to pass on what I've been taught as I studied and interceded for the fellowship gatherings of God's people.

Tried and time-tested truths of Scripture are the basis of any study. It's important to approach teaching the Scriptures with honest hearts, nothing personal to prove, and no audience to please. The approach for this study is based on four basic premises.

1. The Holy Spirit inspired the Scriptures, and we depend on the Holy Spirit to interpret the same.
2. Scripture interprets Scripture. This is context. Not only in context of the chapter, but every truth must be weighed in light of the whole Bible.
3. Historic context. How did the people who were hearing the word or prophecy understand it? This is the least reliable means of interpreting because it's not possible to fully walk in their sandals. We may get part of how they heard it but rarely the whole picture.
4. We do not interpret the Bible based on our experience. Our view of life and time is short sighted and not a reliable arbiter of truth.

Some readers may question whether what is taught here is an idealistic kind of Christianity. My response is that it is no more idealistic than a goal post on the football field. We may not be there yet, but it's time to put the offense on the field and battle our way toward the goal line. The benefits of Christian gatherings are too awesome to give up the goal and punt the ball to the opposing team.

The first book of the Kalmus Series, *Great Separations*, taught about being separated from darkness and brought into the light of Christ. When we are separated from darkness to walk in the Light, we are ready for *Great Gatherings in Jesus' name*. The goal of this study is to inspire Christians to strengthen their faith by encouraging them to join with others in worshipful assemblies.

Part I
Gather the Grain, New Wine, and Oil

Then I will send rain on your land in its season, both autumn and spring rains, so that you may gather in your grain, new wine and olive oil.
(Deuteronomy 11:14)

Chapter 1
The Great Departure

Key Scriptures:

- "When he [Jesus] saw the crowds, he had compassion on them, because they were harassed and helpless, like sheep without a shepherd." (Matthew 9:36)

- "'Woe to the shepherds who are destroying and scattering the sheep of my pasture!' declares the Lord." (Jeremiah 23:1)

Today's Christians are in agreement on one thing: there is an urgent need to fix the modern-day church. We see Christian ministries of all stripes in decline. We must ask ourselves, "Does a church in decay really matter in a post-Christian culture?" A majority of this generation have given up on church. But does this make any significant difference in their lives? Our family and community life revolve around the softball team, soccer games, and weekend family outings. But isn't this a good thing? Sunday morning and church are no longer the most important part of the week, and who has even noticed or cared?

In this chapter, we'll examine ourselves and bring our weaknesses to light so we may confess our sins and overcome them in Christ. What are these faults that impoverish us? Our gatherings have become tainted with meaningless traditions1 and swayed by our transient likes and dislikes. Our personal preferences put us in danger of violating God's purpose for assembling. The prophet Amos warned the people of his day how the Lord God felt about their polluted gatherings.

> *I hate, I despise your religious festivals; your assemblies are a stench to me.*
> (Amos 5:21)

Repentance and forgiveness of these sins provide a solid foundation to build upon for the rest of the study, where we will discover the great gifts and benefits we receive as the Good Shepherd gathers us as the sheep of His pasture.

> *Know that the Lord is God. It is he who made us, and we are his;*
> *we are his people, the sheep of his pasture.*
> (Psalm 100:3)

Were the "good old days" really so great? We have to chuckle when we

---
1. Mark 7:7–8.

look back. Grandma and Grandpa grew up in a different world. They took their weekly bath on Saturday night. On Sunday morning they got dressed in their best duds, piled into the freshly washed and waxed family station wagon and spent the best part of their day at church with like-minded friends. They never heard a lawnmower on Sunday, and no one dared rake leaves on the Lord's day. They couldn't swing by the grocery store to get last-minute things for Sunday dinner—a "closed" sign hung in the window. It seems a bit quaint to look back at how everything from personal hygiene, schedules, commerce, and community life revolved around church. It's nostalgic to think about the past. But that day is long gone, and we must live in the present reality. Thank goodness people can shower every day.

This study isn't meant to establish a tenor for the whole study book, but rather to show the need to confess our sin and build a foundation of repentance[2] as we go forward. Our wrong attitudes show a great need for contrition, and Jesus Christ offers us hope in forgiveness and mercy. When people do not reverence Christ as Head of the church, they can't accept the call to submit themselves to any authority.[3] Too many people are not teachable. A rebuke will not be tolerated. No one is allowed to correct us. Because of this, God's people are not equipped to do the work of the Great Commission.[4] But with repentant hearts and forgiveness, we can go forward with confidence to build upon the Rock, Christ Jesus, who is the Head of the church. To understand the challenges, we will look at different generations, opinions, and attitudes the church must deal with to break down the barriers.

It's important to understand the DNA of today's generations. What makes them tick? What is important to them? Employers have to change their hiring strategies and benefit programs to suit this new generation of workers. Retail merchants are forced to change the way they do business to survive in an environment of rapid change. Cars become smart, banks are connected, advertising has modernized, cell phones manage and control our lives, houses are smarter, and the whole world shifts right under our feet. So why can't the church update itself? We can do the church thing on our cell phones, right? We live in a technology driven world, so why not?

American culture and society change so fast we can't keep up. As a nation, we've become more secularized and less religious. The things that society values have changed. Today's prevailing thinkers want public policy to be based exclusively on science; everything must first be verified experientially. We will no longer accept what Creator God established at the beginning

---

2. Hebrews 6:1.
3. Ephesians 5:21.
4. 2 Timothy 3:16–17.

as foundational truth because it doesn't match our experience. We search for wiggle room in the tenets of Scripture if we search at all. We reject the ancient paths[5] as passé. Instead, human logic and science are our gods. Because of this, Christians are confronted with social pressures that demand the church affirm secular values that are inconsistent with our faith.

Listen to the new generation's words: "No one's gonna tell me what to do with my body." "Who do they think they are to tell me I have to walk like Jesus and talk like Jesus?" "You can't be serious. Only one way to God? You're so narrow minded." "The Gospel isn't even logical." "That's not what *I* believe." And then, there are the walking wounded of this generation who say, "I'm trying to recover from church." It's all too obvious that the very foundation of American culture has shifted, and attitudes toward Christianity have experienced a dramatic turn. Modern-day pastors and teachers bear much of the guilt for this change. The Gospel message has been compromised with human reasoning and cultural relevance. But those who compromise the true meaning will be brought to shame.

> *I will bring on you everlasting disgrace—*
> *everlasting shame that will not be forgotten.*
> (Jeremiah 23:40)

What can we do when behaviors, culture, and technology change right before our eyes? Do we just wring our hands as we read the statistics about contemporary churches and our post-Christian culture? When we hear that eighty percent of our churches are in decline, do we simply bemoan this fact over Sunday brunch with our friends? When we hear that churches are dying of old age, do we point fingers at the Millennials? When we drive by the soccer fields filled with kids on our way to church, do we just grumble about their priorities? Is it Grandma's and Grandpa's job to complain to each other over doughnuts and coffee that none of their kids or grandkids ever show up for church? We appease each other with comforting words: "Oh well, we had them baptized as infants." "We had them dedicated when they were still babies—so they're okay, I guess."

Boomers like their church the way it is. It's a comfortable group of friends. They have learned to trust everyone in their little gathering, and they do church the way they've always done church. They sing some worship songs, hug a bunch of friends, stay awake for most of the sermon, shake the pastor's hand, and then share some coffee and cookies in fellowship time. Most importantly they get out the door in time to get a table at their favorite restaurant before the other church people show up.

---

5. Jeremiah 6:16.

Should the church adapt to the attitudes and values of new generations? Should it affirm this modern-day society and its values? Why couldn't the church bend a little and modernize? To answer these questions, it may help to look at what the church is up against in the here and now.

People in this postmodern culture seldom identify with a religious group or denomination. They feel disconnected from church organizations, and because of this they feel no loyalty. Few things are sacred to them, and they will not be bound by imposed dogmas and doctrines.

The Centennials, Millennials, and Generation X have serious complaints about church organizations. They see the church as judgmental. Leaders are too rigid or even abusive. They feel like churches are not inclusive enough. Church programs demand too much of their time and resources—and what do they get in return? It gets even worse if we only look at the dark side of church history. This short-sighted view leads to claims that God and His church are the cause of all our problems.[6] Today's generation turns their back on religion with disdain. "They're all messed up, so why should the church tell me what I can do with my body?" "How can a bungled-up church tell me how to live my life?"

The American family may be at the root in the decline of active Christian and church identity—or is it the other way around? Does the Christian church decline when home life regresses, or does family weaken when we no longer come together in Christ? Should the household unit provide a spiritual foundation and be a place where religious instruction begins? Should dad and mom serve together as priests in the family, to teach and train the children in the disciplines of Christian life? Are they called to lead their children in "paths of righteousness" by reading and teaching the holy Scripture while their own lives reflect Christ? Or are these just idealistic expectations? The answers to these questions will help us see that the decline of our post-Christian culture is often caused by a lack of godly parental leadership at home. This void is reflected in the decline of the American church.

To further the deterioration, upcoming generations have been schooled to be very eclectic in what they believe. They are not provided with foundational truths but left to decide what is right or wrong on their own. They grew up hearing boomboxes blast out: "Feelings, wo-ooo, feelings." Whole generations sink into a spiritual quagmire where they must decide what's right without any direction. To sort it out, they ask themselves: "Does it meet my needs?" "Does it serve to enhance my life goals?" And if not, "I don't need it."

---

6. Recommended reading: *Under the Influence: How Christianity Transformed Civilization* by Alvin J. Schmidt.

Public education and community life contribute to enforce American secularism. Free- thinking people teach that church and state must be totally separate, rather than teaching the constitutional principle of religious freedom. The first amendment has been unofficially amended. It's no longer understood as written: "Congress shall make no law respecting an establishment of religion, or prohibiting the free exercise thereof." Instead the amendment is commonly misunderstood to mean that no visages of religion are allowed in the public square.

Boomers must take their share of responsibility for this decline. This generation made the church irrelevant to life in the trenches. They have given their children a church that wears a religious mask. Today, Christian spirituality is like a miles-wide river that flows with inch-deep water. It is rare for this generation's parents to be committed to live every day with God's word to light their pathway. The church has refused to teach hard truths from the Bible. We proclaim a "feel good" religion. It's a warm, fuzzy gospel. Our churches serve up baby food that has no meat in it. The church attempts to be too culturally hip and off-beat. People are entertained rather than brought to the light of Christ. The church, too often, mimics American culture that doesn't hold to the values of the Kingdom of Heaven. We have given our children and grandchildren a church that depends on human tradition and cultural philosophies.[7]

Too many Boomers have used the church to control people's lives by teaching:

Do not handle! Do not taste! Do not touch!
(Colossians 2:21)

Church elders have become business managers, when their call is to teach people to grow in grace and knowledge. The local church is left burdened with millions in debt to build monumental facilities, and then services are limited to a Sunday morning event and culturally relevant church programs.

Boomers are handing down religious organizations with multiple challenges for the next generation, and their progeny are not interested in a fix. So how will church make a comeback? Everyone knows church is broken but we can't agree on a fix. Will it work to go back to church like it used to be in the first century? Are house churches the answer? Is evangelicalism the answer? Is modernizing the answer? Is a hip church culture the answer? Can we reclaim the great church movements from the past? Will God once again spark a great awakening in this generation? If we made all churches like yours, would

---

7. Colossians 2:8.

that fix all that's amiss? We have more questions than answers, but the reality is that we're not even asking the right questions. We can't fix church—it's mission impossible. We don't have the answers and we can't agree on a remedy. The need for repentance is as obvious as the nose on Cyrano de Bergerac's face. But there is no grief over the ruin of the church. We are no different than ancient Israel who didn't grieve over their ruin.[8]

> *To overcome our failings, we must go forward to the beginning.*
> *In the beginning was the Word, and the Word was with God,*
> *and the Word was God.*
> (John 1:1)

The church must push forward and call people to Christ who is the Alpha and Omega, the beginning and the end.[9] The Omega always brings us back to the Alpha. He is the answer to all our questions. We are called to lift up Jesus Christ. He will call each new generation to His fold. He will call His own to come and gather, no matter if our lives are messed up. We must echo Jesus' call and have a "come as you are" gathering to ask forgiveness before the throne of grace and receive of His abundant salvation, mercy, and forgiveness. Those who answer the call will find rest upon the Rock, Christ Jesus who is "the same yesterday, today, and forever."[10] Christ Jesus works in and through His people by the power of the word and the power of the Spirit, and He will once again bring us to gather together so that we may come into the fullness of Christ. We ought to listen to the prophet Joel's trumpet call.

Blow the trumpet in Zion, declare a holy fast, call a sacred assembly.

Gather the people, consecrate the assembly; bring together the elders, gather the children, those nursing at the breast. Let the bridegroom leave his room and the bride her chamber.
(Joel 2:15–16)

We would do well to echo this call to repentance. Our need for atonement is no less today than the people of Joel's day.[11] It's important to note who the prophet called to assemble with repentant hearts. Parents were to come leading their children by the hand. The trumpet signaled for mothers to come with their nursing children. Even the newlyweds were to come out of their chambers to join the assembly when they heard the trumpet blast. And most of all, the elders and leaders were to join the sacred assembly. Joel's prophetic words called the community to gather. His all-inclusive call makes it clear for us today that the sin of one will stain the whole body of Christ—from babies

---

8. Amos 6:6.
9. Revelation 1:8.
10. Hebrews 13:8.
11. Leviticus 23:27.

to seniors. We can never claim to be without sin until the whole body is glorified and made pure in Christ.

With a foundation of repentance, forgiven and cleansed, we find peace as we gather. Our relationship with the heavenly Father is restored. The heavens are no longer like brass when we pray. Once again, we may enter His gates with thanksgiving and His courts with praise. We can stand in His council, and we are welcomed to dwell in His dwelling. As we live in keeping with repentance, we will see the powerful effect of gathering together to strengthen and prepare us for the good work our Lord Jesus has given us.

With contrite hearts, we are called to separate ourselves from the crowds that walk on a broad pathway. Ours is a narrow way, and few will find it.[12] In the following chapters of this study, we will answer the questions: Why are Christian gatherings of great benefit to us? How do they strengthen us and prepare us for our mission in life—an impossible mission?

1. The Great Departure
Q & A

1. What weaknesses do you see in churches today?

2. What is necessary to reverse the decline in the number of people who participate in worship assemblies?

3. What are the benefits we miss out on when we neglect worship gatherings and fellowship?

4. Do communities of faith need to do something different to attract people in a postmodern culture?

---
12. Matthew 7:14.

My Journal Notes:

Chapter 2
Gathered in His Name

Key Scriptures:

- "For where two or three gather in my name, there am I with them." (Matthew 18:20)
- "And again he says, 'Here am I, and the children God has given me.'" (Hebrews 2:13)
- "'And gather the entire assembly at the entrance to the tent of meeting.' Moses did as the Lord commanded him, and the assembly gathered at the entrance to the tent of meeting." (Leviticus 8:3–4)

"In my name" is the key phrase in Matthew 18:20. But what is in Jesus' holy name? His name is not like a surname, but a revelatory name, a promise, and a gift. God's nature is to reveal Himself in His holy name. To know the Lord Almighty by name makes our gatherings much more than a get-together to sing about Jesus, teach Bible stories about Jesus, and have a discussion on what we think about Jesus. "In my name" is more than a conclave of those who agree with our faith. As Christians it's vital to our spiritual well-being to understand the power, beauty, majesty, and authority of His name. The full effects of His name are awesome to consider.

At the sound of Jesus' holy name, the doors to worship are flung open so we may enter into His presence and hear His words of eternal life. When we have heard and come into agreement with His promises, we in turn minister His words of saving grace to those who gather with us. An assembly in His name opens the door so we may receive the ministries of Jesus, our High Priest. The Scriptures offer a word picture of His love that draws us:

> *Keep me as the apple of your eye; hide me in the shadow of your wings.*
> (Psalm 17:8)

First, as we gather, and then as we are sent out, Christ Jesus ministers to us and through us in the power of His name. His name is a call for all to assemble who are called as the firstborn and enrolled in heaven.[1] And like a brood of hatchlings under the shadow of His wings, all the blessings in His name linger over us. His name enlightens us as we gather, encompassed in the living and active presence of our Lord Jesus Christ. Christ's body, the church, under the authority of Christ, and by the anointing of the Spirit of Jesus, serves to touch those whom Jesus touches and speak Jesus' words to those who

---
1. Hebrews 12:23

will hear.

This study topic comes in four parts. The first is on the dynamic effect of Jesus' name, especially in our gatherings for worship. Second, we will explore how Jesus' name gives us the power and authority to minister and serve in our assemblies and in our communities. The third study offers a perspective of the mind of Christ and His name that compels us to do the work of the kingdom of heaven. And finally, the fourth study delves into the majesty, mystery, and beauty of His holy name.

> Our prayer: O Lord, open our eyes to see the majesty and glory of your holy name, and the name you have given to us.

Study Part I: The Dynamic of Jesus' Holy Name

This topic offers a glimpse into the dynamic of Jesus' holy name in our gatherings. An understanding of this truth is important because we have been given His name, and we are called to come together with Him to minister and serve in accord with His name and in the power and authority of His name.

In His acts of creation God revealed His holy name as Yĕhovah 'elohiym.[2] Before He revealed His name as Creator of all heaven and earth,[3] darkness and chaos encompassed this globe. Then the Word of creation spoke, the Spirit of the Lord God hovered over the waters, and light was separated from darkness to bring order out of chaos. From day one of creation through all of time to the revelation of Jesus Christ, the power and authority of His name has not changed and will never change. Like the Word of creation, when we gather in Jesus' name, He provides order in our worship. His holy name draws us together in love and harmony. By His holy name God's people are all brought into covenant with the Word of creation.

The importance of God's name is also evident in the Genesis account of Abram (Abraham) and Melchizedek. First, we must set the scene to get the significance of this historic account. After Abram drove pegs in the ground to pitch his tents in Canaan, the Lord God summoned Abram to look to the north, south, east, and west. Father God renewed His promise to Abram.

All the land that you see I will give to you and your offspring forever.
(Genesis 13:15)

Then Abram built an altar to the Lord God in that place. It was customary for the kings of the clans and tribes in this land to go to war in the springtime. They conquered and plundered the cities and villages to subject the people to tribute. The monarchs would form alliances to do battle. The spoils to the victorious! They seized the sheep, goats, cattle, all their stored-up crops, and everything of value. This included people. Children would be enslaved.

Abram's nephew, Lot, was captured and carried away as one of the spoils of war. But a man who escaped came to tell Abram, who then called his trained fighting men to pursue the raiding parties. Abram defeated the allied rulers and recovered his nephew Lot, his family, and all the possessions of the conquered people. After Abram's victory, Melchizedek, king of Salem, came out to meet him.

---
2. Genesis 2:4.
3. Romans 1:2.

Melchizedek brought bread and wine and served them to the victor. He was priest of "God Most High." He blessed Abram as if pouring God's holy name upon him.

> *And he blessed Abram, saying, "Blessed be Abram by God Most High,*
> *Creator of heaven and earth. And praise be to God Most High,*
> *who delivered your enemies into your hand."*
> (Genesis 14:19–20)

Then in verse 22, Abram raised his hand before the Lord God and spoke out God's holy name to affirm his oath. "With raised hand I have sworn an oath to the Lord, God Most High, Creator of heaven and earth."

Melchizedek came to bless Abram in the name of God Most High, Possessor[4] of heaven and earth. In the thousands of years since, God's name has not changed. God's holy name is the power of victory, the power to bless, the power of provision; indeed, His name is all sufficient for every need. His holy name bestows authority to uphold His promise. There is healing in His name. And by the authority of God's sovereign name, Abram's name became Abraham, father of nations. His new name became a constant reminder of God's promise.

Hundreds of years later Abraham's descendants were enslaved in Egypt. God's people were subjected to the lashes of cruel taskmasters. The burden on their shoulders was more than they could bear. The slave driver's whip cut into their backs, and they called out to the Lord in their misery. They were an enslaved nation in a land of strange speech. But they cried out to the God of Abraham, Isaac, and Jacob, and the Lord of Hosts heard their plea. Then as the Lord God prepared Moses to deliver His people and gather Israel as a nation, Moses asked a crucial question about God's name, and then by the power of His name, God changed the course of a nation.

> *Moses said to God, "Suppose I go to the Israelites and say to them,*
> *'The God of your fathers has sent me to you,' and they ask me,*
> *'What is his name?' Then what shall I tell them?"*
> *God said to Moses, "I AM WHO I AM.*
> *This is what you are to say to the Israelites:*
> *'I AM has sent me to you.'" God also said to Moses, "Say to the Israelites,*
> *'The Lord, the God of your fathers–the God of Abraham, the God of Isaac and the God*
> *of Jacob–has sent me to you. This is my name forever,*
> *the name you shall call me from generation to generation.'"*

---

4. There is a strong implication in this Hebrew word קָנָה qânâh; meaning "bought," as in blood bought.

(Exodus 3: 13–15)

We, like the tribes of Israel, have been enslaved.[5] Today our cruel taskmaster is the darkness of sin. The burden of our sin crushes us, the chains hold us down, and our sin is like an evil tyrant that dominates. But we have a great hope. Our hope is in the name of the Lord God. In the bondage of sin, we cry out and call on His name—God Most High, Creator of Heaven and Earth who is Lord and Savior. God Almighty provided a Deliverer. Our loving Father, the Great I AM, sent His one and only Son, Christ Jesus as the promised Yeshua HaMashiach.[6] We are gathered as a holy nation in the name of Jesus the Christ, our Lord and Savior. The Apostle Peter wrote to the church:

> *But you are a chosen people, a royal priesthood, a holy nation, God's special possession, that you may declare the praises of him who called you out of darkness into his wonderful light.*
> (1 Peter 2:9)

The rich and beautiful ministries of the Word and the Spirit of Jesus wash over us like a flood. We gather together to receive of the ministries of His holy name. How is it possible to describe the majesty and glory of His holy presence that permeates our gatherings in His name? We have a sense of His presence as the saints come together to worship, and yet many still yearn to recognize His presence. With this desire in our heart, there is a crucial question we must ask. Who is this awesome Head of the church? What is His name and what are His titles?

> Our prayer: May our hearts and souls yearn to know the true nature of your holy presence as revealed in your holy name. May our eyes be opened to see the beauty, majesty, and power of Jesus' holy name like watching the petals of a rose bud open to the morning sun.

Look to Jesus Christ our High Priest, the One who is ever present as we gather. He is the Almighty One who is King above all kings[7] and Sovereign over all rulers and leaders of tribes, cities, states, and nations. He establishes kings, rulers, and elected officials. He deposes leaders, and rulers of nation-states. He is Lord over all the heavens and the earth,[8] and there is no one who even compares with Him.[9] There is no power in heaven or on earth that is able to come near to Him.[10] Our Lord Jesus, who is present with us, is Son of the Most High God[11] in

---

5. Titus 3:3.
6. Meaning: Jesus the Messiah.
7. Revelation 17:14.
8. Philippians 2:9–11.
9. Psalm 40:5.
10. Colossians 2:15.
11. Luke 1:32.

whose splendor our knees buckle and we must bow in reverent submission.[12]

The presence of Christ enters our gatherings as the Light of the World,[13] and the Light of Life.[14] He sheds glorious light into our hearts and souls to drive out the darkness that would destroy us.[15] He is present with us as the beginning and end of all.[16] Christ Jesus, who spoke the word and all creation came to be, comes to gather with us.[17] By His sure promise we become heirs of eternal life[18] so we may dwell with Him forever.[19] The Anointed One, Yeshua HaMashiach, gathers us to prepare our hearts for when we will see Him face to face.[20]

Christ Jesus is the One who abides with us.[21] He is the Bridegroom who prepares His bride.[22] He pulls down strongholds[23] that are barriers to His goodness and mercies. He stands together with us as the Author and Perfecter of our faith.[24] The only Son of God,[25] Creator of all heaven and earth comes among us as Counselor,[26] Everlasting Father, and Prince of Peace.[27] In His presence, He shows us the way to life, peace, and rest.[28] He comes as a servant and ministers to the people of His flock as our great High Priest.[29] His holy presence lifts us up to worship in His heavenly sanctuary.

But you have come to Mount Zion, to the city of the living God, the heavenly Jerusalem. You have come to thousands upon thousands of angels in joyful assembly, to the church of the firstborn, whose names are written in heaven. You have come to God, the Judge of all, to the spirits of the righteous made perfect, to Jesus the mediator of a new covenant, and to the sprinkled blood that speaks a better word than the blood of Abel.
(Hebrews 12: 22–24)

Too often we limit our view of Jesus as only a teacher. Some regard Him as a great prophet who walked among us here on the earth for a while, but now He's gone. We rescind the power of His name on our behalf if we use it only as an incantation, as if Jesus was our custom-made god. These viewpoints relegate people to spiritual poverty because they deny the fullness,

---

12. Philippians 2:10–11.
13. John 9:5.
14. John 8:12.
15. Ephesians 5:8.
16. Revelation 22:13.
17. Colossians 16:17.
18. Romans 8:17, Titus 3:7.
19. Psalm 27:4.
20. 1 Corinthians 13:12.
21. John 15:4.
22. Isaiah 61:10.
23. Isaiah 60:16.
24. Hebrews 12:2.
25. Matthew 3:17.
26. Isaiah 9:6.
27. Isaiah 9:6.
28. John 14:6.
29. Hebrews 4:14.

majesty, power, and ministries of His holy presence. Too often, we see the Holy Scriptures as great literature and lyrical masterpieces by ancient authors but miss the living, active presence of the Word. We miss the reality of His holy name when we turn the story of Noah and the flood into beautiful, illustrated children's story books about a man who gathered the beautiful animals two by two. In reality, it's an account of God's just and righteous judgments against sin and of His abundant grace and mercies to those who call on His name.

Now is the time to know the Father in the reality of Christ in our gatherings. He has revealed Himself to us by His name. Enter into the richness of His holy presence with the congregation in the fullness of His name. His wonderful name is given to us for His good purpose.[30] His name is your family name. His name is conferred upon all who are baptized into Christ because we are the children of promise.[31]

> *Come, let us bow down in worship, let us kneel before the Lord our Maker;*
> *for he is our God and we are the people of his pasture,*
> *the flock under his care. Today, if only you would hear his voice.*
> (Psalm 95:6–7)

---

30. Ephesians 2:10.
31. Romans 9:8.

Study Part I
The Dynamic of Jesus' Holy Name
Q & A

1. What existed before God revealed Himself as Creator of heaven and earth?

2. Describe the power and authority of God's holy name.

3. How do God's people steal away the power of Jesus' name?

4. Describe the presence of Christ Jesus, our High Priest, who joins with us in our gatherings.

My Journal Notes:

Study Part II: Minister in Jesus' Name

The glory, power, majesty, and beauty of the name of our Lord Jesus Christ affects everything we do as we gather in His holy presence. His name stirs us to minister, and the Holy Spirit anoints, gifts, and empowers us to serve. In the presence of Christ Jesus, our cups overflow with rivers of righteousness from the throne of God so that we may worship, serve, and minister before the Lord of all heaven and earth.

Who is the Lord God in whose name we serve? We must know His name because as we step up to serve, like the Old Testament priests, we ascend the steps to the Holy Place. We enter the sanctuary to receive of Christ's ministries, and then minister as priests—to speak what He speaks and touch those He touches.[32] For people of faith, two, three, or more of us join together and come up into His holy presence. Shoulder to shoulder,[33] we go up to Mount Zion, to the city of the living God, the heavenly Jerusalem to join thousands upon thousands of angels in joyful assembly.[34] Indeed, when we worship, serve, and minister in His name, holy angels minister to us in Jesus' presence, and we ought to be familiar with His name.

How is it that God's people are given authority to minister in Jesus' name? A symbol of this authority in the Scriptures is a signet. Pharaoh gave Joseph a signet as a sign of authority. Joseph's word became as good as Pharaoh's when he wore the signet with the king's name engraved on it. When Joseph spoke, it was as if Egypt's ruler spoke.

In the book of Esther, the king gave Mordecai a signet with authority to write and seal dispatches using his name. He exercised this authority to save God's people. David ruled Israel in the authority conferred upon him by the King of kings. The God of Israel instructed David to pass this authority on to his son, Solomon. The Lord Almighty declared that He would make Zerubbabel, "like my signet ring, for I have chosen you."[35]

By means of Jesus' Great Commission command, we too are given a signet. By means of His command we minister in His authority. As His disciples we're called to serve in Jesus' name just as He serves. We're ordained to reach out and touch those whom Jesus touches. We're commissioned to go where He goes to proclaim the Gospel, preach the Good News, and baptize in the name of the Father, and the Son, and the Holy Spirit. We call out to broken people so we may anoint them with Jesus' healing oil. In Jesus' name we weep

---

32. 1 Peter 2:5.
33. Zephaniah 3:9.
34. Hebrews 12:22.
35. Haggai 2:23.

with those who weep and mourn with those who mourn.[36] Those bound by the chains of sin are set free. We search with love and compassion for souls who wander. We lead them to Christ Jesus who joins them to the True Vine[37] so they can produce good fruit. We do all this, submitted to Christ and by means of the authority of the Head of the church, our Lord Jesus Christ.

God's appointed governor, Zerubbabel, laid a foundation to rebuild God's holy temple for His name.[38] God's redemptive work continued into the era of the church. The Apostle Paul compelled the church in Corinth to be built upon Christ, the foundation, with gold, silver, and costly stones.[39] What is to be built with this precious building material? Christ Jesus is the Master Builder of the church,[40] and He has commissioned us as precious building stones and workers on His construction crew. We see a picture of this in 1 Kings 5:3–5. The Lord God, Yĕhovah, commissioned Solomon to build a temple for the "Name of the Lord." The phrase "Name of the Lord" is repeated three times in these verses to underscore that the temple is to be built for His holy Name—the triune God. Why use this phrase with emphasis rather than say, "build a temple for the Lord" as written in 1 Kings 6:1?

The reason is simple and beautiful. The Lord's holy nation in the Old Testament was called by His name. He conferred a name on them to gather them as His own unique people. They built the temple as a gathering place for all who were called by His name. His name brought together the priests, prophets, kings, princes, carpenters, millers, merchants, farmers, mothers, fathers, children, and infants—all who were in His name. This foreshadowed the church of today that we are called to build. Together we are built into the temple of His Holy Spirit.

Keep in mind that the church isn't a building with a cross on it. Nor is it a space in a strip mall, a basement recreation room, a warehouse, or an auditorium. The church is not a brick and mortar structure. Instead the church is all of us together who are called in Jesus' Name to gather in Christ who is Head of the church. His holy Name makes church come to life in us. We are the precious stones to build His holy temple—the church.

This temple is built upon the Rock, the Chief cornerstone, with living stones.[41] Jesus' Great Commission gives us authority to make disciples and baptize them into Christ, in the name of the Father, and the Son, and the Holy Spirit. We welcome all who will come to Christ in our gatherings

---

36. Romans 12:15.
37. John 15:1.
38. Zechariah 4:9.
39. 1 Corinthians 3:12.
40. Matthew 16:18.
41. Psalm 118:22.

because God's assembled people are the place where the Lord of Hosts is present. The temples' construction crew works to make room for all those who come to saving faith.

> *Enlarge the place of your tent, stretch your tent curtains wide,*
> *do not hold back; lengthen your cords, strengthen your stakes.*
> *For you will spread out to the right and to the left.*
> (Isaiah 54:2–3)

Who gave us the authority for this work? What is His name? All Jesus' disciples have cause to stand tall because we are sent in the name of the Great I AM. We are called to serve the One whose name is above all names, Immanuel, who is God with us.

> *Therefore God exalted him to the highest place*
> *and gave him the name that is above every name.*
> (Philippians 2:9)

We administer the Bread of Life because that is His name. We serve to call God's people to be partakers of the cup of Him who is the Lamb of God whose shed blood takes away the sin of the world.[42] We minister forgiveness, mercy, and cleansing from sin in the authority of His holy Name. When we gather together in His name at the Lord's Table to partake of His body and His blood in holy remembrance, we enter into His holy presence with angels in a miraculous "joyful assembly."[43]

His name is Messiah, Christ, to all who receive the gift of His saving grace. His name reveals that He is the Righteous Judge who judges with justice in all righteousness. Because we know His name we can come before Him, knowing Christ is our eternal hope—our only hope. We are called to minister and serve in the name of Jesus who is Prophet, Priest, and King. He is first above all prophets, the High Priest of the church, and Prince of Peace. He is the first and greatest Apostle of the church. Our calling is in Jesus' name, who is the Door: the way, the truth, and the life.

Stand tall, armor up, step into authority in His Name. You have been given His signet of authority to minister and serve before Him. We lift up His holy name so that all may hear and know our Lord and Savior.

> Our prayer: With our hearts overwhelmed with gratitude, thank you Father for revealing the glory of your presence to your sons and daughters through your holy name.

---

42. John 1:29.
43. Hebrews 12:22.

It overwhelms us as we come to know God's nature. His character compels Him to reveal Himself to a weak and fallible people. He opens the hearts and minds of His sons and daughters so we may know Him by name. To all who come to know His name, their knees will bow, tongues will confess, and hands will lift up in worship and praise. We gather to worship in His name, but what is the name that compels us and inspires us to gather and worship?

Consider the power, majesty and glory of each name and title of the One who gathers us in His holy name. It's important for each of us to know with whom we gather. Is He Jesus our Teacher? Jesus the Prophet? Oh, yes! But so much more. Let us enter into the fullness of Christ as one—together.

Christ the Head of the church is our Advocate.[44] He advocates on our behalf and pleads our case before our Father in heaven. He takes our prayers, petitions, and our heart's cry before the throne of grace to represent our cause. He is Mediator[45] who knows our weaknesses because He has walked the same path we have walked, and He mediates on our behalf to reconcile us to our heavenly Father. He is Righteous Judge[46] who knows the hearts of the saints and judges with grace and mercy. He is Authority[47] as Head of the church, and He confers this authority in our gatherings to provide us with godly order.

The Head of the church in whose name we gather is Messiah, the Promised One[48] to deliver us from the bondage of sin, to lift the burden of sin. He is Deliverer[49] from the power of death that once held us in its powerful grip. He is Jesus our eternal hope, and the Prince of Peace[50] who throws down the barriers that divide us. He crushes the walls of hostility that separate us. In Christ who is Hope,[51] we are made to be one body—the church. The One who gathers us is Prophet[52] above all prophets who speaks to the people to reveal Himself and the glory of His name.

We gather in the name of our Redeemer.[53] All things will be brought under His feet, and He will stand on the earth victorious. There is great and fearsome power for all who are gathered in Christ, the Resurrected One.[54] He broke the power of darkness and death that held us captive, and now He

---

44. 1 John 2:1.
45. 1 Timothy 2:5.
46. Acts 10:42.
47. Matthew 3:17, Titus 2:15.
48. John 1:41.
49. Romans 11:26.
50. Isaiah 9:6.
51. Ephesians 2:14.
52. Mark 6:4.
53. Job 19:25.
54. 1 Corinthians 15:3–4.

gathers us to Himself in freedom and light. In the resurrected Christ, we are lifted up in a great and awesome strength with mighty effect in our gatherings.

> *For thus says the One who is high and lifted up,*
> *who inhabits eternity, whose name is Holy:*
> *"I dwell in the high and holy place,*
> *and also with him who is of a contrite and lowly spirit,*
> *to revive the spirit of the lowly,*
> *and to revive the heart of the contrite."*
> (Isaiah 57:15)

As a community we come into the living and active presence of our Lord and Savior. His Gospel is preached, taught, and proclaimed to reveal to us our need of Christ and His saving grace. He is the Door,[55] the Way[56] to saving faith, the only Son of the Living God, Creator of all heaven and earth. He is Truth;[57] the plumb line of truth,[58] and the standard of truth. There is no truth apart from Him.

Faith compels us to be productive as we assemble by the power of the word. Together we bear the good fruit of the vine because we are grafted into the True Vine.[59] As we gather in Jesus' holy name, we come into the presence of Jesus who rises up as Healer.[60] There is healing in His spoken word to restore our souls. His touch heals us and enlightens us. Body, soul, and spirit are restored in His holy name, because God who Heals us is His name.[61] We come together with the Giver of all good gifts,[62] and when we hear God's word and come into agreement with the Gospel truth, He confirms the truth with the ministries of spiritual gifts administered in the authority of His holy name.

This is the power of the Name that gathers us together to receive the ministries of our High Priest, Jesus Christ. Enlightened in the light of His name, we gather to be hearers and doers of the word,[63] and to worship, serve, and minister in His name.

---

55. John 10:9.
56. John 14:6.
57. John 8:32.
58. Amos 7:7.
59. John 15:1.
60. Malachi 4:2.
61. Exodus 15:26.
62. Ephesians 4:8, James 1:17.
63. James 1:22.

Study Part II
Minister in Jesus' Name
Q & A

1. How does a gathering for worship inspire and empower us to serve?

2. How is the authority to minister in Jesus' name given to us?

3. Describe the building stones of the church.

4. Which of Jesus' descriptive names or titles inspires you most of all?

My Journal Notes:

Study Part III: Serving with the Mind of Christ

It takes a change of the heart to serve with the mind of Christ. Our Savior's love changes our hearts and inspires us to acts of service. It's like, throw aside that swanky suit or that fancy silk blouse, roll up our shirt sleeves and bend our knees to wash dirty feet. An application of Jesus' example is found in repentance, because in this way we serve to cleanse life's dirt from the feet of our brothers and sisters in Christ. This is the heart of a servant.

When we serve in the manner of a foot washer, with our knees and back bent, this is the mind of Christ. But our default human mindset is to desire greater things than to be a lowly foot washer. We are tempted with grandiose thoughts. It's almost cliché to say, "Of course I would give up my life for the cause of Christ." When we say this, we don't ever expect to be faced with death threats in America where we have constitutional religious protections. We make a grand statement to say we'll give up our lives for our faith, but we shun serving with the attitude of a foot washer. It's a common human weakness to desire a position of authority to lord it over others. But this attitude must be avoided at all cost because we are called to be Christlike servants.

Mary, mother of Jesus, gave us a beautiful example of the heart of a servant. God's angelic messenger, Gabriel, came to her and announced:

"You will conceive and give birth to a son, and you are to call him Jesus.
He will be great and will be called the Son of the Most High."
(Luke 1:31–32)

When she heard the name of the child she would bear, her heart was humbled, and she replied with humility:

"I am the Lord's servant," Mary answered. *"May your word to me be fulfilled."*
(Luke 1:38)

After Mary became pregnant by the power of the Holy Spirit, she traveled to visit her relative, Elizabeth. When she heard Mary's greeting, the child leaped in her womb. Mary responded with a prophetic song.

My soul glorifies the Lord and my spirit rejoices in God my Savior,
for he has been mindful of the humble state of his servant.
From now on all generations will call me blessed.
(Luke 1:46–48)

The power of the name becomes evident in Mary's story. She humbled herself with the heart of a servant, to serve God's holy purpose that He established in the beginning, in Genesis, for the redemption of humankind from the bondage of sin. When she knew her child's name, Isaiah's prophecies washed over her like a flood.

> *Therefore the Lord himself will give you a sign.*
> *Behold, the virgin shall conceive and bear a son,*
> *and shall call his name Immanuel.*
> (Isaiah 7:14 ESV)

Immanuel was born, walked among us, was crucified, buried, and raised from the dead, to become Head of the church that is His body. As Jesus ascended to heaven, He gave His followers a work to do in His name and with His attitude. We are to walk in Jesus' sandals with the mindset of Christ who is our Head.

Who is this Jesus, and how are we called to walk? We know Him by His name; we gather in His name; and as we walk in His footsteps, we will see the power in His name. Our hearts are humbled to come into His living, active presence to worship, serve, and minister in His name.

What is the name of the One in whom we worship, serve, and minister? As ambassadors, it's as if we present our credentials by saying, "I have been sent in Jesus' holy name." There is power in the name, authority in the name, victory in the name, forgiveness in the name, and an ever-flowing abundance in the name. We have great confidence as we gather together to be sent out in His name. To know the heart of Christ is to know His presence. Press on in this study to know the fullness of His name.

Study Part III
Serving with the Mind of Christ
Q & A

1. What does Mary's response to the angel Gabriel reveal about her heart's attitude?

   _____
   _____
   _____

2. Describe the abundance of Jesus' name.

   _____
   _____
   _____

My Journal Notes:

Study Part IV: The Majesty of His Holy Name

To further open our hearts to the names of the One in whose name we gather, and the effects of His presence, we'll look in more detail at the name of our Lord God who is present with us as we gather. All too often, we suppose Christ's presence and don't understand the fullness of who He is in our midst. The reverence and awe of Christ's living and active presence as revealed in God's name will affect our gatherings for an eternal good. As we become familiar with each of His names, we come closer to the heart of God, and nearer to the heart of worship.

Deliverer: This is the name of Christ who delivers us from the chains of sin and rescues us from God's just and righteous wrath against sin that might otherwise destroy those He has called to be His own sons and daughters.

> *With awesome deeds of justice you will answer us,*
> *God our Deliverer; you are the confidence for everyone at the ends of the earth, even for those far away overseas.*
> (Psalm 65:5 ISV)

> *You turned to God from idols to serve the living and true God, and to wait for his Son from heaven, whom he raised from the dead–Jesus, who rescues us from the coming wrath.*
> (1 Thessalonians 1:9–10)

Faithful and True is our Savior's name. The Lord Almighty is true to every promise. He fulfills every word down to the last little punctuation mark. We can trust His word that He will never leave us nor forsake us, because He is faithful even when we are not.

> *I saw heaven standing open and there before me was a white horse, whose rider is called Faithful and True. With justice he judges and wages war.*
> (Revelation 19:11)

He is faithful to bring all those who have been given to Him just as He safeguarded His disciples.

> *"I protected them and kept them safe by that name you gave me. None has been lost except the one doomed to destruction so that Scripture would be fulfilled."*
> (John 17:12)

Good Shepherd is our Lord's name. His shepherd's rod and staff guide to keep us safe in the flock He has gathered. When we wander away, He searches until He finds us. He will never abandon us even when we wander from the pathway where He leads us.

"Suppose one of you has a hundred sheep and loses one of them. Doesn't he leave the ninety-nine in the open country and go after the lost sheep until he finds it? And when he finds it, he joyfully puts it on his shoulders and goes home."
(Luke 15:4–6)

"I am the good shepherd. The good shepherd lays down his life for the sheep."
(John 10:11)

Holy Servant is the name of our Savior. Jesus instructs us to be like-minded, especially as we are gathered together in His holy name. With hearts and minds of servants we are all one in Him.

"Now, Lord, consider their threats and enable your servants to speak your word with great boldness. Stretch out your hand to heal and perform signs and wonders through the name of your holy servant Jesus."
(Acts 4:29–30)

Who, being in very nature God, did not consider equality with God something to be used to his own advantage; rather, he made himself nothing by taking the very nature of a servant, being made in human likeness. And being found in appearance as a man, he humbled himself by becoming obedient to death—
even death on a cross!
(Philippians 2:6–8)

Victorious One: The gathering that established the church, as recorded in the book of Acts, stands as a great victory in the history of all humankind. Christ victorious, the Head of the church, now seated at the right hand of the Father, is given a scepter to rule and reign on high. Though He reigns above, He is present with us wherever He gathers us in victory.

To the one who is victorious, I will give the right to sit with me on my throne, just as I was victorious and sat down with my Father on his throne.
(Revelation 3:21)

But about the Son he says, "Your throne, O God, will last for ever and ever; a scepter of justice will be the scepter of your kingdom." (Hebrews 1:8)

Lord God Almighty: What a magnificent name, El Shaddai. As God prepared to gather a nation as His own people, He spoke His name to Abram, "El Shaddai." God has not changed and as He gathers us together, He is to us the great I AM, God Almighty.

> *When Abram was ninety-nine years old, the Lord appeared to him and said,*
> *"I am God Almighty; walk before me faithfully and be blameless."*
> (Genesis 17:1)

The Most High God: Melchizedek, the king and priest of Salem, came out to meet Abram, the victor over his enemies. He declared God's name to Abram, El Elyon. And then, as he blessed him, he offered bread and a cup of wine—a supper that bound them in fellowship. Because the Lord is the Most High God, in Jesus' name we gain the victory over sin and death so we may come together as overcomers in our gatherings in Jesus' name.

> *"Blessed be Abram by God Most High, Creator of heaven and earth.*
> *And praise be to God Most High, who delivered your enemies into your hand."*
> (Genesis 14:19–20)

God of Covenants: Creator God made covenants with Adam and Eve, Noah, Abraham, King David and his lineage, and an everlasting covenant of peace with all who are called by His holy name. The church is established in covenant with Christ. God's covenants are relational covenants that bind us together as one with Him in a bond of love. The impact of the blood of the eternal covenant is the power of resurrection that raised up the "great Shepherd of the sheep."[64]

> *"Though the mountains be shaken and the hills be removed, yet my unfailing love for*
> *you will not be shaken nor my covenant of peace be removed,"*
> *says the Lord, who has compassion on you.*
> (Isaiah 54:10)

> *Give ear and come to me; listen, that you may live.*
> *I will make an everlasting covenant with you,*
> *my faithful love promised to David.*
> (Isaiah 55:3)

---

64. Hebrews 13:20.

Master: Our Lord God is Sovereign over all of creation. There is nothing outside of His domain. This is Adonai in whose name we gather to worship, serve, and minister. He is Master over the heavens and earth, and in holiness He comes together with us as High Priest of our assemblies in His name. Like Abram, by faith we find hope in the Master of all creation.

> *But Abram said, "Sovereign Lord, what can you give me since I remain childless and the one who will inherit my estate is Eliezer of Damascus?"*
> (Genesis 15:2)

Jehovah: The Lord God began to reveal Himself to the patriarchs in their time. Now the church has a better covenant, and Yahweh has revealed himself in greater measure to those who gather in His holy name to hear His holy word read, taught, and proclaimed: "So that you may know that you have eternal life."[65]

> *This is the account of the heavens and the earth when they were created, when the Lord God made the earth and the heavens.*
> (Genesis 2:4)

> *God also said to Moses, "I am the Lord.*
> *I appeared to Abraham, to Isaac and to Jacob as God Almighty,*
> *but by my name the Lord I did not make myself fully known to them."*
> (Exodus 6:2–3)

The Lord My Banner: When we are gathered together in Jesus' name, Jehovah Nissi is our Banner. He covers us with a banner of love. His banner is a battle standard, a flagstaff on a mountain that draws us to Him to make us ready to fight the good fight.

> *Your troops will be willing on your day of battle. Arrayed in holy splendor, your young men will come to you like dew from the morning's womb.*
> (Psalm 110:3)

> *Moses built an altar and called it The Lord is my Banner.*
> (Exodus 17:15)

> *Let him lead me to the banquet hall, and let his banner over me be love.*
> (Song of Songs 2:4)

---

65. 1 John 5:13.

The Lord who Heals: Blessed be the name of the Lord, Jehovah Rapha who heals body, soul, and spirit. Moses wrote, "If you," as a condition for God to heal the tribes of Israel. For those who gather in Jesus name, by the work of the cross He has fulfilled every "If you," and in the righteousness and truth of His holy presence He is the Lord who heals you.

> *He said, "If you listen carefully to the Lord your God and do what is right in his eyes, if you pay attention to his commands and keep all his decrees, I will not bring on you any of the diseases I brought on the Egyptians, for I am the Lord, who heals you."*
> (Exodus 15:26)

The Lord Is There: In our gatherings where the Gospel is preached, the redeemed are baptized, and God's people are welcomed to the Lord's Table, Jehovah Shammah is there with us. When we gather in Jesus' name, He is faithful to be present. The barriers have been torn down by means of the cross of Jesus Christ, and our High Priest makes us holy so that He may usher all those He gathers into God's holy presence. Ezekiel prophesied as he looked forward to the time when the curtain will be torn, and in Christ we will have access to worship before Jehovah Shammah.

> *"And the name of the city from that time on will be: The Lord is There."*
> (Ezekiel 48:35)

The Lord Our Righteousness: God's people are called to righteous deeds, but we can't attain a righteousness of our own. Jehovah Tsidkenu is our righteousness. Our Lord Jesus Christ fulfilled all righteousness and confers His righteousness upon those He has called and chosen. Christ Jesus gave us His name, and because we are called by His name, we have assurance that we are the righteousness of God in Jesus Christ. In the light of His righteousness, we now have fellowship in the body of Christ and cleansing by the blood of Christ.

> *This is the name by which he will be called: The Lord Our Righteous Savior.*
> (Jeremiah 23:6)

> *My dear children, I write this to you so that you will not sin. But if anybody does sin, we have an advocate with the Father–Jesus Christ, the Righteous One.*
> (1 John 2:1)

The Lord Who Sanctifies: We come to the cross of Jesus Christ just as we are—weary, burdened with sin, and in need of a Savior. With our knees bowed in repentance we are washed with saving grace. Now justified, we come to Jehovah Mekoddishkem who sanctifies us. We are made holy in Christ, and then it's a lifetime project to make all that we do conform to His holiness. He accomplishes this by the power of the word and the convicting work of the Holy Spirit. Every gathering is a kind of Sabbath rest leading us to sanctification.

"Say to the Israelites, 'You must observe my Sabbaths. This will be a sign between me and you for the generations to come, so you may know that I am the Lord, who makes you holy.'"
(Exodus 31:13)

"Come to me, all you who are weary and burdened, and I will give you rest."
(Matthew 11:28)

The Everlasting God: When we come into a gathering in Jesus' name, we enter the realm of the eternal, and El Olam is present with us. The water and the word of Baptism have an eternal effect on those gathered. The bread and cup of the Lord's table are a supper with an eternal impact on our lives. The Gospel that is sung, taught, preached, and ministered to change lives for eternity. The tree that we planted in our backyard may live long after we have passed on, but God is Everlasting.

Abraham planted a tamarisk tree in Beersheba, and there he called on the name of the Lord, the Eternal God.
(Genesis 21:33)

Creator God: The awesome work of creation Elohim accomplished in seven days would take human intellect many lifetimes to comprehend. Creator God established all that exists, and it was good. He set the sun, moon, stars, and planets in their places, and established the foundations for family, culture, and governments. The laws of nature were set in place, and He completed His creation by entering His rest—a place for us to dwell with Him forever.

In the beginning God created the heavens and the earth.
(Genesis 1:1)

The Lord Will Provide: The darkness of impoverished souls is driven back in the light of Jehovah Jireh, God who Provides. The greatest of all provision is the Lamb of God who takes away the sin of the world. By faith, Abraham looked forward to the day His Messiah would come to establish a new covenant by the blood of the sacrificial Lamb. In His light, every need is provided for us in this lifetime as well, for everyone whether good or not.[66]

> *So Abraham called that place The Lord Will Provide. And to this day it is said, "On the mountain of the Lord it will be provided."*
> (Genesis 22:14)

The Lord Is Peace: "Peace, peace!" Everyone cries out for peace in this upside-down world, but will they look to the Prince of Peace? Jehovah Shalom is all sufficient for those who look for an end to chaos and violence. Taking up a placard to march in protest will never get us together in one accord. The end of all strife, a true and lasting peace can only be found in the Lord our Peace. By means of His holy name we will see the day when swords will be beaten into plowshares and spears into pruning hooks.[67]

> *So Gideon built an altar to the Lord there and called it The Lord Is Peace.*
> (Judges 6:24)

> *"Peace I leave with you; my peace I give you. I do not give to you as the world gives. Do not let your hearts be troubled and do not be afraid."*
> (John 14:27)

The Lord of Hosts: When we come into the presence of Jehovah Sabaoth, a holy awe will wash over us. As God manifests Himself, we will be like Isaiah and the Apostle Peter who suddenly became aware of their sinfulness. Gathering together in the fullness of His presence, where the Gospel is opened to us, we will know the Lord of Hosts who comes to be present with us. Our eyes will be opened, and we will see our need of Christ, our Lord and Savior to receive of His grace, mercy, and forgiveness.

> *"Woe to me!" I cried. "I am ruined! For I am a man of unclean lips, and I live among a people of unclean lips, and my eyes have seen the King, the Lord Almighty."*
> (Isaiah 6:5)

---

66. Matthew 5:45.
67. Isaiah 2:4.

> *When Simon Peter saw this, he fell at Jesus' knees and said,*
> *"Go away from me, Lord; I am a sinful man!"*
> (Luke 5:8)

Jealous God: The fire of God's jealous protection are flames that we want to surround us. The blaze of Jehovah Qanna's abundant love is greater than the protective love of a mother for her newborn child. God's heart is toward His sons and daughters, and He fiercely protects against those who would steal our hearts away.

> *Do not worship any other god, for the Lord, whose name is Jealous,*
> *is a jealous God.*
> (Exodus 34:14)

> *For the Lord your God is a consuming fire, a jealous God.*
> (Deuteronomy 4:24)

God who Encompasses: Jehovah Tsûwr is God who binds all of us together as one in Him. God Almighty is before us, behind us, and surrounds us with His grace, love, and mercies. He lifts us up and sets our feet upon the Rock to protect us, and then safeguards us and shows hostility toward our adversaries.

> *You have encircled me; you have placed your hand on me.*
> (Psalm 139:5 CSB)

God the Father: With the heart of Abba Father, God spoke to proclaim Jesus as His Son. With the same heart, Father God will adopt you as His own whom He loves. The love of Abba Father is fully manifested in Christ Jesus who is present with us as we gather in His name.

> *He received honor and glory from God the Father when the voice came to him from the*
> *Majestic Glory, saying, "This is my Son, whom I love;*
> *with him I am well pleased."*
> (2 Peter 1:17)

> *Jesus answered: "Don't you know me, Philip, even after I have been among you such a*
> *long time? Anyone who has seen me has seen the Father."*
> (John 14:9)

The richness of Christ's presence is revealed in His holy name. For those who desire to know the strength, power, and authority of Christ in times of community worship it's vital to welcome Christ as Lord of all, as revealed in His name. We must not be like Pharisees who claimed to know the Father but refused to recognize Jesus as their Yeshua HaMashiach. We walk in pharisaical footsteps if we say, "I love my Savior, I enjoy the Comfort of the Spirit of Jesus, but I don't want any of that church stuff." We show our divided hearts when we claim the name of Christ Jesus and say we submit to Christ but submit to each other? "No way!"

We have an impoverished religion if we only welcome Jesus as a Christmas baby in a manger but refuse to accept that He is the Righteous Judge who will rule over His enemies with an iron scepter.[68] We are in danger of creating a Jesus in our own image when we accept Jesus as Redeemer but despise[69] or forbid[70] His spiritual gifts that strengthen the church. Those who say they believe in Jesus but refuse the baptism He commands, or trivialize remembrance of Him at the Lord's Table, have a custom-designed Jesus of their own making. Some may claim the comfort Jesus sends by His Spirit but can't accept that He cures sickness in our time. A pick-and-choose kind of faith is not consistent with Jesus who rises up with healing in His wings.[71] When we claim a part of Jesus' nature but reject another part, we're in danger of keeping company with those who believe He was a great teacher but not the resurrected Lord and Savior.

We ought to be true to His name because the name is worthy of all glory, honor, and praise. Like Jesus who walked among us, we ought to delight in the fear of the Lord[72] because of His holy name. This holy reverence and awe will lead us to enter into the full beauty and majesty of His presence. The joy of His name will well up from within us and overflow like a river of Living Water.

Where two come together in Jesus' name there will always be three, because our Lord Jesus is present in His fullness as revealed in His holy name. Father God gathers His sons and daughters to assemble in the tent of meeting where Jesus comes to minister as High Priest.

> *Do you not know that your bodies are temples of the Holy Spirit,*
> *who is in you, whom you have received from God?*
> (1 Corinthians 6:19)

---

68. Revelation 2:27, 19:15.
69. 1 Thessalonians 5:20.
70. 1 Corinthians 14:39.
71. Malachi 4:2.
72. Isaiah 11:1–3.

In Jesus' name, the doors of worship are flung open to welcome all who are called to gather as the sheep of His pasture. The sheep know the Good Shepherd's voice and come together as He calls them so He may minister to them. By means of the power and authority of His name, Jesus our High Priest makes us holy and reconciles us to the Father so we may worship Him in spirit and truth. In the name of Christ, we are privileged to gather together to worship in the Most Holy Place, to bow in His presence, to stand in God's council, and to dwell in the Father's dwelling place.

Jesus' holy name reveals the Father as all-sufficient in every circumstance and for the needs of the gathered sheep of His pasture. God's splendor and majesty are revealed in His name, and we are humbled to come together to exalt His name. Immanuel, God with us, began His ministry with the disciples by saying, "Follow me," and before He ascended to heaven, He wrapped up His work with the disciples, saying, "Follow me." This remains a call for the priesthood of all believers to gather with the flock, to minister, and serve in Jesus' name. A gathering in Jesus' name makes people of all stripes into one body, where:

> *There is neither Jew nor Gentile, neither slave nor free,*
> *nor is there male and female, for you are all one in Christ Jesus.*
> (Galatians 3:28)

We are brought together to minister with the mind of Christ, which is the heart of a servant, not to exalt ourselves above others.

We are provided with an abundance of spiritual blessings as revealed in Jesus' holy name. Our soul and spirit will prosper as we come into the fullness of Christ. To escape our spiritual, religious poverty, we are called to welcome all of our Lord Jesus as He reveals Himself to be in His holy name. We relegate ourselves to an impoverished spiritual rut when we treat His holy name like a buffet, accepting what we like and rejecting what we don't.

Gather together in the fullness of Christ our High Priest to be a hearer and doer of God's word. Receive of the abundance of Spirit of Jesus that is gifted to us as we gather together in Jesus' holy name. Learn and know His name to build in your heart an eager anticipation of the fullness of His presence in the assembly of His body, the church, in the tent of worship. Gather together in Jesus' name so we may ascend to the heights like the feet of a deer.[73] God's people come together to receive of the ministries of our High Priest, and then the blessed gathering follows us with every step we take, everywhere we go. To know our Lord God, to be on familiar terms with Christ, we must know His name.

---

73. Psalm 18:33.

Study Part IV
The Majesty of His Holy Name
Q & A

1. How does the revealing of our Lord and Savior's descriptive names and titles bring us closer to God and to the heart of worship?

2. Does Jesus' name change how you respond when you gather with others to worship and serve?

3. What is the effect of picking and choosing what we like about Jesus Christ?

4. Describe in your own words the beauty and majesty in the names of our Lord and Savior.

My Journal Notes:

Chapter 3
In the Presence of our High Priest

Key Scriptures:

- "We have such a high priest, one who is seated at the right hand of the throne of the Majesty in the heavens, a minister in the sanctuary and the true tent that the Lord, and not any mortal, has set up." (Hebrews 8:1–2 NRSV)

- "Praise the Lord. Praise the name of the Lord; praise him, you servants of the Lord, you who minister in the house of the Lord, in the courts of the house of our God." (Psalm 135:1–2)

In this study, we will come to see Jesus as our High Priest who ministers His living, active presence in our gatherings. The goal is for the hungry to receive the Bread of Life, and for the wanderer to hear the Good Shepherd shout out his name. Our purpose is to enter into true and real worship, and to lift up holy hands to exalt the Lord in the presence of Jesus, our High Priest.

For he satisfies the thirsty and fills the hungry with good things.
(Psalm 107:9)

Where is the place we are called to gather? Can you locate it on an online map? How is this sanctuary built? What, or who, are the living stones? How is it possible to ascend to this place of worship when we sit uncomfortably on a hard-oak bench, or on a padded chair that's too comfortable? Can a gathering of Christians know when Jesus Christ is present to minister?

These are good questions for anyone who desires to sit at the feet of our Lord Jesus to hear words of grace and comfort. To enter His presence we ascend, like the feet of a deer on a mountain.[1] They are beautiful songs of the heart that also encourage us to gather as saints so that we may hear and do what our High Priest teaches. When we receive the truth of the Gospel, we are empowered in worship, service, and ministries of the living active presence of our Lord and Savior, Jesus Christ.

With contrite hearts, ears to hear, and a teachable spirit; come, let's tabernacle together.

A mysterious reality becomes evident when God's children are gathered in Jesus' name. We enter into the presence of our High Priest who is Jesus the Christ. We ascend into His holy presence, the sanctuary, the true tabernacle

---
1. Habakkuk 3:19.

of worship where our Lord Jesus ministers. The author of Hebrews reveals this spiritual reality.

> *But you have come to Mount Zion, to the city of the living God, the heavenly Jerusalem. You have come to thousands upon thousands of angels in joyful assembly, to the church of the firstborn, whose names are written in heaven. You have come to God, the Judge of all, to the spirits of the righteous made perfect, to Jesus the mediator of a new covenant, and to the sprinkled blood that speaks a better word than the blood of Abel.*
> (Hebrews 12:22–24)

Many of the first Christians gathered together in hidden caves. Today some disciples must huddle together in illegal house churches. In other corners of the world, mud huts with thatched roofs provide Christ's followers with shelter for their assembly. And still others gather in sparkling glass cathedrals or stained glass and carved stone structures. Each of these are tangible spaces, but there is a greater glory. When God's people come together in Jesus' name, we ascend to worship on Mount Zion, to the city of the living God to assemble with the holy angels where Jesus our High priest ministers. Look at the original Greek in Hebrews 8:1–2 to see an awesome truth.

In the key Scripture, "sanctuary" is the Greek: hágios, hag'-ee-os. The meaning is "Most holy thing, a saint." The word "tabernacle" is skēn , skay-nay'; that means a "tent or cloth hut—habitation, tabernacle." Remember that the Apostle Paul refers to our body as a tent.

> *For we know that if the earthly tent we live in is destroyed,*
> *we have a building from God,*
> *an eternal house in heaven, not built by human hands.*
> (2 Corinthians 5:1)

The author's amplified paraphrase of Hebrews 8:1–2 will help us understand: "We have such a High Priest who is seated at the right hand of the throne of Majesty in the heavens, who serves in the sanctuary of saints, the true tent of His habitation the Lord has made, not built by human effort." Jesus' followers tend to seek tangible things when they don't see the reality of heaven's spiritual realm. We search for material things we can touch and see with our eyes. What we see with the human eye and touch with our hands may remind us of the Kingdom of heaven, but it is temporary and external. It will come to an end. There is an invisible realm that is a greater reality than what we can perceive with natural senses. This unseen reality is where the sanctuary our High Priest, Jesus Christ, ministers and serves those who gather together. Of course, we see real people in our gatherings. We may see beautiful stained-glass illustrations of Biblical truths. We may also see gilded crosses and inspirational banners, and these are good things in their place. But the sanctuary we cannot see with the human eye is built with living stones, and it is a greater reality. The precious stones are the saints of God, who are the eternal sanctuary not made by human hands. This is the One to whom we ascend as we gather in Jesus' name—our High Priest who ministers His living and active presence to all who will come and sit at his feet.

Consider the psalms of ascent. They are beautiful refrains that rang out to call God's people to gather in Jerusalem at the Temple of worship where their high priest served. Worshipers would chant these psalms as they traveled up the narrow, dusty path along the cliffs from Jericho to Jerusalem. Mothers, fathers, and children would sing out as they ascended from Bethlehem to the holy city. The priests sang these psalms as they ascended the fifteen steps to where they would minister in the temple.

I rejoiced with those who said to me, "Let us go to the house of the Lord."

> *Our feet are standing in your gates, Jerusalem.*
> (Psalm 122:1–2)

Moses built the Tabernacle tent according to the pattern shown to him on the mountain. The Temple Solomon built in Jerusalem foreshadowed Christ. The people ascended to worship on the holy mountain where the Temple served as a model of what is in heaven.[2] And now, because we have a better covenant, we enjoy the reality of Christ. We have a tabernacle of worship not constructed by human hands.

Our sanctuary is not aloft in the distant heavens. Its foundation is not dug into the earth. It is not restricted by geographic limitations or national boundaries. True worship cannot be limited by denominational labels or by the name painted on the church marquee. Of course, various Christian faiths have established paradigms and traditions of worship, but all too often they are "built by human means." We must not allow our worship to be constrained by external practices, religious labels, or brick and mortar.

> *However, the Most High does not live in houses made by human hands.*
> *As the prophet says: "Heaven is my throne, and the earth is my footstool.*
> *What kind of house will you build for me?"*
> (Acts 7:48–49)

When God's people genuinely gather in Jesus' holy name, they are set free from the divisive limitations that build walls between them. Human rea-

---

2. Hebrews 8:5.

soning no longer holds them down. They will ascend to worship in a temple not made by human hands—a tabernacle that is a gathering of saints, and the habitation of our High Priest, Jesus Christ. In faithful gatherings we come to dwell in the fullness of Jesus' living and active presence. Worshipers will rise above human confines to a sanctuary that is not limited by the visible, temporal world around us. This heavenly center of worship is built with eternal precious stones upon the solid Rock, Christ Jesus. Again, this place of worship is not made by human hands, nor is it any part of this material creation.

He has entered that greater, more perfect Tabernacle in heaven, which was not made by human hands and is not part of this created world.
(Hebrews 9:11 NLT)

When Christians gather, are we called to ascend to the heavens above us? Is this temple of worship located somewhere in God's vast created universe? These questions come from temporal-spatial thinking. The gathering place is in the kingdom of heaven, and Jesus' instructions give us a clue to its whereabouts. When Jesus sent His twelve disciples to minister in the authority of His name, He instructed them:

"As you go, proclaim this message: 'The kingdom of heaven has come near.'"
(Matthew 10:7)

Jesus was asked when God's kingdom would come, and He answered:

"The coming of the kingdom of God is not something that can be observed, nor will people say, 'Here it is,' or 'There it is,' because the kingdom of God is in your midst."
(Luke 17:20–21)

Jesus teaches that the kingdom of heaven is a reality in the spiritual, unseen realm. The church is in this domain, built with precious stones—redeemed souls who gather as building blocks of the church.

The point is clear. When we ascend to gather and worship together in Jesus' name, He is with us. His presence as High Priest is necessary because: Without holiness no one will see the Lord.
(Hebrews 12:14)

We are made holy in Jesus Christ so that we may enter the Most Holy Place to worship and serve. Jesus is not present with us in an ethereal sense. Even though we can't see Him with mortal eyes, His living, active presence washes over us, encompasses us, and overflows from within us. As we come together, we go up into the ministries of the presence of our High Priest, Jesus Christ. Together in spirit we cross a threshold to the heavenly sanctuary, and our Lord Jesus' holy presence floods our souls. This sanctuary is a gathering of saints in His name.

How do we know Jesus, our High Priest is actively present when we gather? The question is like asking, "How do you know when an avalanche roars down the mountain?" Or like asking, "How do you know a mother loves her child?" Jesus is the Lion of Judah,[3] the Lamb of God, and His presence is both dynamic and tenderly loving.

When our spiritual eyes are opened to see the miracle of holy baptism, we will see the water and the word create a new life in Jesus Christ, and His holy presence will be evident. When we gather together to partake of the bread and the cup of the Lord's Table where Jesus Christ ministers forgiveness, restores our souls, makes us whole, and strengthens our spirit—His presence will wash over us and through us like a flood. When Christ and the cross[4] are preached, taught, and believed, the effect is powerful and evident in the lives of those who gather.

We will know our Lord Jesus Christ is present in a gathering when the true Gospel is preached and hearts are brought to repentance. When the Good News is received and believed, we will witness people being separated from the dark side of this world. This is what happened on the day of Pentecost when Peter proclaimed Jesus as the crucified Lord and Messiah.

> *When the people heard this, they were cut to the heart and said to Peter and the other apostles, "Brothers, what shall we do?"*
> (Acts 2:37)

Manifestations of Jesus' living, active presence are also made evident in our gatherings through the ministries of spiritual gifts, given as the Spirit desires. This is more than one gifted person on an elevated platform with a pulpit, sermon notes, and a microphone. Christ Jesus makes His presence evident in and through the priesthood of all believers who congregate. All who gather are made working parts of the whole, and all are called to ministries of spiritual gifts so that His presence is unmistakable.[5] All of Jesus' disciples are called to serve the church in accord with their spiritual gift. An ordained work has been prepared from the beginning of time for all who are called by His name. When we enter into true and real worship, our spirit crosses a threshold into God's unseen kingdom realm. Jesus' presence is manifested when we step over the divide and minister from our spirit, empowered by the Holy Spirit.

We have learned that Christians are called to gather together in Jesus'

---
3. Revelation 5:5.
4. 1 Corinthians 2:2.
5. See author's books on spiritual gifts: Treasures of the Kingdom and A Jewel of the Kingdom.

name to worship and serve. We have entered into the immeasurable and eternal joy, benefits, and blessings of gathering together, and thereby we fulfill our calling. Now we can see why we are called to ascend to His sanctuary and receive the ministries of our High Priest, the Son of the Living God, our Lord and Savior. We see Jesus who is the threshold through whom we enter into God's holy presence. We hear Jesus' welcoming words:

> *"I am the way and the truth and the life.*
> *No one comes to the Father except through me."*
> (John 14:6)

After being convicted in an illegal trial, Jesus' body was lashed, a crown of thorns pressed on His head, His beard was torn out, He was spit upon, and then His hands and feet were nailed to a cruel Roman cross. And when Jesus gave up His spirit, the curtain that separated the Most Holy Place was severed from top to bottom.

> *At that moment the curtain of the temple was torn in two from top to bottom.*
> *The earth shook, the rocks split.*
> (Matthew 27:51)

The Old Covenant divide was torn down to show us there is a new and better way. Jesus is the Gate, the Door, and the Way into God's holy presence.

Jesus' disciples are made holy in our Lord and Savior. They are the body of Christ who is the Head. In Him, as His body, we may enter into His glory. The prophet Isaiah saw this glory:

> *I saw the Lord sitting upon a throne, high and lifted up;*
> *and the train of his robe filled the temple.*
> (Isaiah 6:1)

We enter into the gates of the Holy Place with thanksgiving overflowing from our hearts, and with praise on our lips. We go through the torn curtain into the Most Holy Place by means of the body and blood of Jesus Christ.

> *Therefore, brothers and sisters, since we have confidence to enter the Most Holy Place by the blood of Jesus, by a new and living way opened for us through the curtain, that is, his body.*
> (Hebrews 10:19–20)

When we gather together in Jesus' name, we are covered by the blood of Christ. As the body of Christ, we are provided a way to come:

Near to God with a sincere heart.
(Hebrews 10:22)

Together in His name, Jesus is present with us, and it's possible to know His presence beyond any doubt. Our High Priest's ministries are made evident in so many ways. Jesus' active presence is revealed as the word is taught and preached. His holy presence is manifested as we hear the word. As we gather at the Lord's Table, He is present to minister forgiveness and mercy. In the miracle of baptism, and in the ministries of spiritual gifts, the resurrected Christ is made known. The evidence is not in brick, mortar or stained glass but in precious living stones—the building blocks of His sanctuary.

Where our High Priest serves and ministers there is no place for human reasoning, religious labels, or empty external practices. These things limit true worship in the sanctuary.

Don't you know that you yourselves are God's temple and that God's Spirit dwells in your midst? If anyone destroys God's temple, God will destroy that person; for God's temple is sacred, and you together are that temple.
(1 Corinthians 3:16–17)

Come to the Fountain of Life. Let us tabernacle together in His holy name to receive of the ministries of our High Priest, Jesus Christ! In Jesus' living and active presence, let us worship in spirit and in truth. May our worship be spiritual and real.

In him the whole building is joined together and rises to become a holy temple in the Lord. And in him you too are being built together to become a dwelling in which God lives by his Spirit.
(Ephesians 2:21–22)

3. In the Presence of our High Priest
Q & A

1. Where does Jesus our High Priest minister?

2. In our gatherings, what purpose is served by brick and mortar, stained glass, and inspirational banners?

3. How do we know Jesus' living and active presence is with us in our assembly?

4. What are some of the man-made, divisive limitations imposed on the church?

My Journal Notes:

Chapter 4
Gather to Hear and Do

Key Scriptures:

- "Do not merely listen to the word, and so deceive yourselves. Do what it says. Anyone who listens to the word but does not do what it says is like someone who looks at his face in a mirror and, after looking at himself, goes away and immediately forgets what he looks like. But whoever looks intently into the perfect law that gives freedom, and continues in it—not forgetting what they have heard, but doing it—they will be blessed in what they do." (James 1:22–25)

- "Always learning but never able to come to a knowledge of the truth." (2 Timothy 3:7)

One of the many blessings we are given as we gather together in Jesus' name is to hear God's written word read, taught, and preached. The words we hear are living words that permeate soul and spirit to comfort, strengthen, correct, and make us a people who are motivated by our love of Christ to take action according to what we have heard. This study topic focuses on the power and effect of gathering together to hear God's word so we can meditate on what we hear, and then allow the word to permeate every part of our lives.

Faith is planted in us as we hear what God has spoken in His word—the Bible. This is a great miracle of God's kingdom. The word we hear takes root in our hearts. When the word is combined with faith,[1] it grows and flourishes to show us our need of Christ who is revealed in the Bible from Genesis to Revelation. God's word is like a powerful seed planted and then watered by heaven's rain to grow and spring up in our hearts.

In a Christian gathering, we hear the word as it is taught, preached, ministered, and lived out among us. This is not just about sounds that float into our human ears. It's more like a tsunami wave that washes through us to impact soul and spirit. The effect is to devastate us in our sinful state, bring our hearts to repentance, and then rebuild us in the righteousness of Jesus Christ. With contrite hearts, cleansed of unrighteousness, we are made hearers of the word, and by faith receive it into our soul and spirit. In righteousness we are spurred to act according to the word we hear.

To absorb God's word requires more than human ears that work. Faith comes by hearing the word of God, but it's not a physical process. If it were

---
1. Hebrews 4:2.

natural ears that heard and brought us to faith, a deaf person could not be saved. We know that's not true. Instead, we hear God's word, the Gospel, with the ears of the heart, soul, and spirit. We hear holy words with spiritual ears that strike the heart and show us our need of Christ. Ears of the flesh won't hear the truth. Stephen, a deacon in the early church, decried the unhearing, "uncircumcised" ears of the religious majority just moments before they stoned him to death.[2] The prophet Jeremiah proclaimed the human ear to be unable to hear, and what it does happen to hear, it finds offensive.[3]

The book of James instructs us not to betray ourselves.

Do not merely listen to the word, and so deceive yourselves. Do what it says.
(James 1:22)

It's not like we can simply show up at church and someone reads the holy Scriptures, the sound goes into our ears, and it's a done deal. Going through the motions doesn't satisfy the hunger of the soul. No! We are called to hear with our hearts and add faith to God's life-giving words. This is satisfying to the soul. The Lord's goodness and mercies overtake us when we hear, acknowledge the truth, and act on it.[4] Jesus said:

The words that I have spoken to you–they are full of the spirit and life.
(John 6:63)

The power of God's word will ignite the fire of the Holy Spirit in your heart and affect what your hands, feet, and mouth do. The word is the catalyst that causes you to serve as your part in the body of Christ.

The next step after hearing is to come into agreement. Again, we add faith to God's word, and by faith our hearts and minds come together. We assimilate the word into our everyday lives when we meditate on it and act upon it. This will change how we do our job on Monday morning, our lunch time conversations, and our attitude toward the boss. All we set our hand to do will be changed because of the word we have heard and received when we gathered in Jesus' name.

Have you ever looked at your face stubble in the mirror, then shaved, put on your uniform, and as you drove to work, a flash thought came over you? That guy in the mirror, does he really look like my dad? How quick we are to forget the reflected face we see.[5] But the power of gathering in His holy name to serve, sing, teach, preach, and pray the holy Scriptures is possible because

---

2. Acts 7:51.
3. Jeremiah 6:10.
4. 2 Timothy 3:7.
5. James 1:24.

we are a reflection of Christ. The notes we sing imprint the message in our minds and hearts. Teaching with inspired words of truth causes our faith to grow. Fervent prayers lift our burdens and change our hearts, minds, and circumstances. Then, our meditations go with us as we work with our hands Monday morning. The words, music, the teaching, and prayers will ring in our hearts to strengthen us in soul and spirit so that we may do what the word compels us to do. Ministries of the word in our gatherings serve to make us a reflection of Christ and triggers our memories as we are sent out in Jesus name.

When we are taught the foundational truths of God's word, we are given what is called the "meat of the word," and it's worth taking time to chew.[6] This is true meditation on the word. It's not an "empty your mind" kind of meditation. It is to take time and reflect on God's word. This is thinking through the things we hear in our gatherings. We contemplate the word as if placed alongside our daily lives so we may examine ourselves.[7] We listen as the Holy Spirit simmers what we have heard. When we take time to consider the word ministered to us, it's like we are sent with a brown bag care package in hand to sustain us until we gather again.

This kind of meditation may also be likened to the deer in the forest that chews its cud to help it digest. A deer has four stomachs to break down its food. After chewing, she swallows the food again to pass it to the second stomach, and so on. This example from nature shows the power of reflecting on the word we hear in our gatherings. To illustrate this truth, we will relate the temporal body to the deer's first stomach. The second stomach is compared to our mind. The third stomach is like our soul, and the fourth to our spirit. As we hear God's word with ears of faith and digest it, the word will affect every part or our being.

The first "stomach" of meditation serves to "fill the body with light."[8] We "chew" to meditate so the truths and wisdom of the word will enlighten our body and give nourishment to our bones.[9] By faith, the light of the word brings our temporal being into agreement with the Scriptures. In other words, our flesh is "circumcised" by the power of God's holy word.[10] The effect is that our soul and spirit are empowered to rule over our sinful nature.

Next, as we digest God's word, our mind is renewed, and we are given the mind and attitude of Christ.[11] Our thoughts change, and we focus less on our

---
6. Hebrews 5:12.
7. 2 Corinthians 13:5.
8. Luke 11:34.
9. Proverbs 3:8.
10. Colossians 2:11.
11. 1 Corinthians 2:16.

own ambitions. We will be motivated to serve others with a sacrificial kind of love. Our neighbors will be valued above ourselves.[12] The world around us will be revealed in a whole new light—the light of Christ.

The soul is the third step to absorb the word we have heard. As we digest the milk and meat of the word, our soul is strengthened and brought into agreement with the word. The fourth powerful effect of meditating on God's word is that the Spirit of Christ, by means of the word, strengthens our spirit. As our mind, soul, and spirit come into agreement with the word, we are strengthened to do battle against the world's enticements.[13]

Hearing God's word taught, preached, and prophesied is best accomplished in a Christian gathering. The power and majesty of Christ, the Head of the church, is manifested when we come together in agreement, in the name of Jesus because He is there with us. In community, we are better receptors for the Spirit of Jesus to minister the word to us so we can hear as the word is sung, taught, and ministered. The teaching we hear, the songs that ring out beautiful truths of the kingdom, and the ministries of the Holy Spirit will minister to us in the assembly, and then provide the lunch we carry home to further nourish mind, soul, and spirit.

Let me offer another example to help the farmer and gardener types to understand this truth. The principle of gathering to hear God's holy word is somewhat like planting corn. If you grow one stalk of corn, there can be no cross-pollination. It takes at least two or three stalks of corn for the wind to help pollinate it, and a whole patch of corn is better yet.

In the same way it is best for a whole "patch" of disciples to gather in Jesus' name for the word to "pollinate" and produce good fruit. The wind of the Spirit serves to make the gathering abundantly fruitful. This is the powerful effect of close fellowship in Jesus' Name. As we come together to hear the word, we are spurred to act in accord with God's word. Jesus taught us:

"Now that you know these things, you will be blessed if you do them."
(John 13:17)

Another benefit as we gather to hear God's word is that our daily prayers will be guided, inspired, and informed as we come together in Christ to hear the holy Scriptures read, taught, preached, and prophesied. When we want to pray in accord with God's will, and in agreement with what is right and true, we pray in line with the word we have heard. We pray in agreement with David, the shepherd and king, when we pray the Psalms. Our prayers will

---

12. Philippians 2:3.
13. James 1:14.

agree with our Lord Jesus when we pray in harmony with His prayer for His disciples and for all who are called by His holy name.[14]

There are even more benefits to hearing the word together. Have you ever experienced one of those "can't eat just one" moments? When you hear God's word, you will always have an appetite for more.

Taste and see that the Lord is good.
(Psalm 34:8)

When we gather together with other Christians and the ears of our heart are opened to hear the word, we will find an abundance of refreshing sweetness, and we'll want more. As we partake of the word together in Jesus' name, we will come to desire more of the word—morning, noon, and evening. We'll want to wake up to the word and devour more of God's word as we end our day. The joy and sweetness of the Scriptures we hear will always arouse our appetite for more and more.

The power and effect of gathering together is more than human words can describe. This practice affects our work, play, and community life, and it informs our prayers. When our fellowship time comes to an end, God's goodness and mercies go with us like taking a brown-bag care package.[15] The blessings we receive have a forever quality. By the power of hearing God's word, Christ Jesus the Word comes to life in us, and the seeds of faith are planted and stirred in our heart. When we hear and receive what is taught and preached from God's word, the seed of faith is planted and watered to make the kernels of truth germinate, grow, and flourish in us.

By the power of the spoken word, we are delivered from the demands of our human nature. Our minds are renewed to have the mind and attitude of Christ. Our prayers are informed as we come together to hear God's word read, taught, and preached. A get-together in Jesus' name, where we listen to words of comfort, strength, and healing will always create an appetite for more of the holy Scripture's sweetness. By the power of the word that we hear proclaimed in our gatherings, body, soul, and spirit are brought into agreement. The wind of the Spirit pollinates God's word among those who will hear and apply it to family life, work, service, and ministry. All this is best accomplished as we gather together in Jesus' holy name.

---

14. John 17.
15. Psalm 23:6.

4. Gather to Hear and Do
Q & A

1. Describe the effect of God's word on those who hear the word with ears of faith.

2. What is the significance of Christians being a reflection of Christ?

3. Give an example of meditating on God's word.

4. Why is gathering together to hear God's word the most effective way to grow in grace and knowledge?

My Journal Notes:

Chapter 5
Sanctified in Gathering

Key Scriptures:

- "But you were washed, you were sanctified, you were justified in the name of the Lord Jesus Christ and by the Spirit of our God." (1 Corinthians 6:11)

- "It is God's will that you should be sanctified." (1 Thessalonians 4:3)

Sanctification presents an interesting dichotomy because by our own strength, and by our own actions, we cannot attain godliness. It is only in Christ we are made perfect. And then as this good work comes to fruition in us, the righteousness of Jesus Christ affects everything we do and how we do it. External human efforts toward sanctification stand in opposition to true godliness that can only be accomplished by the Spirit of Christ at work in us. The primary tools He uses to make us like Christ are

1) the anointed preaching and teaching of the truths of God's word,

2) searching and meditating on the Scriptures to know God whom we serve,

3) the ministries of spiritual gifts,

4) the prayers of the saints,

5) ministries of sacraments and ordinances in the church.

Each of the above are best accomplished as we gather in Jesus' holy name.

Sanctification comes to fruition by the power of God's word and in the power of the Holy Spirit. Gathering together in Jesus' name is an effective means of sanctification. In our assemblies we are encouraged to cooperate with the Spirit and the word to grow in grace and knowledge.

When holiness is taught, all too often it is dismissed as moralistic—too judgmental. It's true that when instruction in godly values are dissociated from Christ and the work of the cross, it becomes a form of moralistic deism. The reality of sanctification is that it is not a work of the flesh, nor accomplished on our own. This presents a conundrum, because sanctification is not a work we can do, and yet it's best when we are "all in" as Christ sanctifies us together in our gatherings. Sanctification is not a maverick kind of thing. It's as if we each serve as the sandpaper that God uses to refine our brothers and sisters in Christ.[1]

---
1. Proverbs 27:17.

When the Holy Spirit sows the seed of God's word in someone who has a teachable spirit, it's planted in fertile ground.[2] Searching from the Bible serves to water the seed. Diligent study to test and prove what is taught is like weeding the garden. Meditation on the word is like collecting and preparing our garden's bounty. Our spiritual garden flourishes and bears fruit, and we grow in the grace and knowledge of our Lord Jesus Christ.

Each of the following verses and comments teach us about the result of sanctification in our worship gatherings in Jesus' name. Each point will have a focus Scripture followed by an instructional citation. The comments are presented as seed for a group discussion and individual study.

But if we walk in the light, as he is in the light, we have fellowship with one another, and the blood of Jesus, his Son, purifies us from all sin.
(1 John 1:7)

As Christ sanctifies us, our faith and trust will grow and flourish. It's a bonus that we also learn to trust those who come together to worship, serve, and minister alongside us. Our fellow worshipers may grate on us like sandpaper at times, but we can trust that His beauty will be revealed out of the rough.

When we join this community of light, we enter into a fellowship in Christ. We are called to come into sanctifying fellowship in our Lord Jesus Christ and His body, i.e. the people who gather. In fellowship with one another, we continue to stand under Christ's protective blood covering. We are cleansed by the blood of Christ for the sake of His holy name—all for His glory.

Be devoted to one another in love.
Honor one another above yourselves.
(Romans 12:10)

Bonds of fellowship are a delight to observe. As we gather together, our trust grows; we are bonded together as a family, and a union of love grows and blossoms. The fragrance of this community flows out like the aroma of orchard blossoms in springtime.[3] This is a union that is like threads woven together with an altruistic love. It's like weaving threads of gold with blue, purple, and scarlet yarn, and the finest linens, woven and embroidered fabric created for temple worship.[4] This elaborate cloth is a garment of devoted love to adorn the bride of Christ.[5]

---

2. Hosea 10:12.
3. Song of Songs 4:16.
4. Exodus 39:3.
5. Ezekiel 16:13.

> *Be completely humble and gentle; be patient,*
> *bearing with one another in love.*
> (Ephesians 4:2)

The Apostle Paul admonishes us to do what is impossible. Godly meekness, tender heartedness, enduring concern, and putting up with one another long-term is impossible. We might be able to fake it for a while, but sooner or later it becomes too much to bear on our own. No earth-bound love can make acts of Christlike love possible. These good things are achievable only in the love of Spirit. His love works in us to affect our love for Him and leads us to delight in Him. And then, our love flows out to all who are called to be a part of the body of Christ. This is the fruit of God's sanctifying work in us.

> *Bear with each other and forgive one another if any of you has a grievance against someone. Forgive as the Lord forgave you.*
> (Colossians 3:13)

Can we even imagine the miraculous, joyful worship gathering that we would enjoy if everyone thought ahead to plan for the good of others? As sanctified people, we think less of our own needs and more about the needs of the person who sits next to us. This kind of attitude is earth shaking. When we have the mind of Christ, it will first change the tone of our gatherings, and then flow out to affect our communities, state, and nation.

> *And let us consider how we may spur one another*
> *on toward love and good deeds.*
> (Hebrews 10:24)

When equestrians spur a horse toward a jump, the horse instantly picks up speed and then leaps over the hurdle. The spur doesn't hurt the mount but is used to signal the horse to pick up speed and sail over the hedge.

The author of Hebrews teaches that Christians need to be spurred on to love each other and perform good deeds. It's true. Our human default mode is to settle in, find our comfort zone, and become complacent. We need to feel the spur from time to time to motivate us.

This is not the job of one or two people in the church, but an "one other" kind of activity. This means that all of us are called to serve as encouragers. We are taught to think ahead about ways to inspire each other to loving servanthood in our gatherings and communities.

> *Be completely humble and gentle; be patient,*
> *bearing with one another in love.*
> (Ephesians 4:2)

True humility is not considering ourselves to be like the dirt under the rug. Rather than looking inward, humility reflects outward and upward in all relationships. True humility serves, is kind, peaceful, endures, helps, and is self-sacrificing. It takes an unpretentious heart to stop, listen, and consider what someone says, even when it feels like the other person steps on our toes.

Those who walk in meekness, put aside their personal strengths[6] to step out in the strength of the Lord. This is like tossing aside a favorite polyester jacket and straw hat to step into God's armor. As we humble ourselves, we enter into awesome strength that is not our own. When we come into a gathering of people with this kind of attitude, it refreshes us, changes our lives, and will give us a desire for more sanctifying Christian fellowship.

> *Be kind and compassionate to one another, forgiving each other,*
> *just as in Christ God forgave you.*
> (Ephesians 4:32)

Can we hear the protests of oppressed people? "You're telling me to show compassion? You don't know what he did to me! His cruelty changed my life. I'll never be the same—he took my dignity. I lost my family, my home, and I couldn't focus on my work for months." This kind of harm is all too real. Asking someone to turn around, show compassion, and forgive undeserving people seems a bit crazy, and on our own it's downright impossible. The guy who harmed us is, at best, like the kid who says, "sorry" only because the parents force him to. Do these violent people deserve to be forgiven?

Our hearts and minds change when we're reminded of the day we came to Jesus. He reached out to us in our depravity, and we were freely forgiven. The blood of the Lamb of God cleansed us. In baptism we entered into Christ, His death and resurrection, and we became adopted as sons and daughters of the Most High God. Our souls were restored. Now, in Christ, forgiveness is given to us liberally as we gather around the Lord's Table. In Christ we have access to our Heavenly Father to offer intercessions and prayers. How could we offer any less for those who have harmed us?

> *For the entire law is fulfilled in keeping this one command:*
> *"Love your neighbor as yourself."*
> (Galatians 5:14)

Jesus was asked "Who is my neighbor?" The answer came in the form of a parable about the Good Samaritan.[7] Instead of giving a direct answer to the question, He made the point that each one of us are to be good neighbors.

---

6. Philippians 3:8.
7. Luke 10: 25–37.

If someone has been attacked, be a good neighbor and lift them up. When someone is hungry, go beside them as a neighbor and feed them. For the person who stands out in the cold, shivering, we wrap our coat around them like a neighbor. When someone comes into our worship gathering looking for a place to sit, a sanctified person serves as their neighbor.

Jesus fulfilled the Law, even the part that commands us to love our neighbor. Does that mean we're off the hook? The substance of this command to love as a neighbor is written on our hearts.[8] Because of our love for Christ, and because of the sanctifying effect of hearing the Holy Spirit speak to us through the word of God, we are compelled to be a good neighbor to any and all that we encounter each day. For those who enter into the fullness of Christ and His righteousness, we are affected to be good neighbors. This means that anyone we meet on the street and those who walk into our worship gatherings are welcomed to the neighborhood.

Let us not become conceited, provoking and envying each other.
(Galatians 5:26)

Think back to those precious moments when we are finally alone. It's like, "Whew! I can sit back and read my book with no interruptions." No one to bug us with questions about why and how, this and that. The quiet and solitude seems nice until our hearts begin to yearn for those we love. Then, when we hear the key in the door, we get excited and put our book down. "They're home." We jump up and put aside our personal wants to greet them because of our love for family, friends, and neighbors.

Love compels the sanctified to let go of self-importance knowing that pride builds barriers to relationship. Our devotion restrains us from setting ourselves above others, because self-importance enflames jealousies. Because we desire peace in our fellowship gatherings, we refuse to exalt ourselves. For the sake of harmony, we are instructed to cast aside our self-centered ways and come into our assemblies with the heart of a servant.

Do not lie to each other, since you have taken off your old self with its practices.
(Colossians 3:9)

The need to feel important often leads us to embellish who we are and our past experiences. But there is no need to glorify our prior exploits so everyone knows how much we gave up to be a Christian. Our name listed in "Who's Who" doesn't offer us status in God's kingdom realm. An office wall covered with framed degrees and awards for excellence and personal achieve-

---
8. Romans 2:15.

ments doesn't serve any good purpose in a worship gathering. Instead, we take on the image of Christ, and we come together in truth and in the power of the Spirit of Jesus. Christ strengthens and lifts us up in a bond of love, but a lie destroys fellowship and divides us.

> *Be devoted to one another in love. Honor one another above yourselves.*
> (Romans 12:10)

The theme is consistent in all our study Scriptures on this topic. When we lift others up, consider them better than ourselves, focus on other people's gifts and talents, encourage someone else in their calling, and work toward the good of the whole body of believers, this is a great expression of devotion to Christ and selfless love toward our Christian family.

> *Live in harmony with one another. Do not be proud, but be willing to associate with people of low position. Do not be conceited.*
> (Romans 12:16)

By the world's standards we have an upside-down kingdom. The Apostle Paul wrote to the Corinthian church to remind them that most of the people drawn to Christ were not the world's great thinkers or from high-ranking aristocratic families.[9] Most often, the Good Shepherd gathers the weak, poor, downtrodden, and the despised of this world. Jesus' first disciples were simple fishermen, and the Great I AM raised up a holy nation out of an enslaved people.

> *May the God who gives endurance and encouragement give you the same attitude of mind toward each other that Christ Jesus had.*
> (Romans 15:5)

We are called to love each other the same way Christ has loved us. Our High Priest of the church strengthens us to endure for the cross of Jesus Christ. By the power of His word and the Holy Spirit, He encourages us in righteousness. His words are health and healing for our bodies. His tender touch heals our broken hearts and restores our crushed souls. Our Lord nourishes us at His table to strengthen us in soul and spirit. God provides all our daily needs. He hears our petitions and answers in a way that He knows is best.

This kind of love is infectious. His love affects how we serve our brothers and sisters in Christ. It's as if the heart, mind, and attitude of Christ sifts into our heart and soul to spread His righteousness to everyone with whom we rub elbows.

---

9. 1 Corinthians 1:26.

> *Hold them in the highest regard in love because of their work.*
> *Live in peace with each other.*
> (1 Thessalonians 5:13)

How should we respond when we overhear someone "roast" the pastor or elders after they have ministered to the people faithfully? This kind of godless chatter is contrary to peace. Whining complaints tear us apart rather than bind us together. Pointing fingers at our leaders discourages those who are called to serve among us.

Instead, we ought to offer encouragement to everyone who does their part to serve in our assemblies. All of Jesus' servants have weaknesses to overcome. D. L. Moody butchered the English language in his preaching. John Wycliffe rocked the boat too many times and was removed from office. Martin Luther suffered with episodes of depression. William Tyndale was deemed obnoxious as he relentlessly pointed out the truths of God's word. The church branded John Huss as a "ring-leader of heretics" because of his stubborn opposition to the wrongs of the church. Many of Christ's servants have paid a high price for their "weaknesses." They were persecuted and many were made martyrs of the church.

We need a lot of reminders that the laborers in our gatherings are God's servants and not ours to judge.[10] They are fallible people. They suffer with us in the same human miseries. We are all in the same boat, with common human weaknesses to overcome.

Even when the failings of those who serve are all too apparent, we are to encourage them in what is right. When our teacher stumbles to find the right word, pray for them. When their remarks offend us, they unconsciously ignore us, or unwittingly brush us off—our love for them ought to serve as a cover.[11] Instead of putting them down, we are taught to "hold them in the highest regard." We should lift them up, serving as ministers of peace in our assemblies.

> *Let no debt remain outstanding, except the continuing debt to love one another,*
> *for whoever loves others has fulfilled the law.*
> (Romans 13:8)

If love could be weighed and measured on a balancing scale, and the imbalance charged as debt, each of us would have an impossible liability to pay. The Apostle Paul instructs us to continue paying this debt of love. It may feel as if we shell out only a few nickels on a multi-million-dollar obligation, but

---
10. Romans 14:4.
11. 1 Peter 4:8.

take heart, love is a currency that multiplies itself.

Creator God loved us first with a love as vast as the universe, and He inspires us to love Him with our whole heart. Our Lord Jesus loves us with a love greater than all the oceans. Because of this, we overflow with His love to our brothers and sisters in Christ and to everyone around us. The flood of His love provides the abundance we need to pay the immense debt we owe for His love. For those who are in Christ, when we pay this debt of love, it's like a mortgage banker who sends us the money to make our house payment every month.

Our Lord Jesus fulfilled the Law by means of His abundant love. In Christ's love shown to others, we too fulfill every requirement of the Law.

> *Therefore let us stop passing judgment on one another. Instead,*
> *make up your mind not to put any stumbling block or obstacle*
> *in the way of a brother or sister.*
> (Romans 14:13)

It's human nature to pass judgment on other people. When we focus on other people's flaws and failures this distracts us from our own problems. We can feel better about ourselves and forget our own failures when we use other people like a stepping stool to elevate ourselves. When we judge others, we can say, "See, I'm not so bad. I don't do that."

Because of our fallible nature, we need to be reminded to stop passing judgment on those who worship with us. The reason is simple. Self-righteous thoughts erode the bond of fellowship. Judgmental attitudes create barriers to love and unity. A worship gathering is neither the time nor place to judge because judgmental attitudes tear down bonds of love and fellowship.

> *Accept one another, then, just as Christ accepted you,*
> *in order to bring praise to God.*
> (Romans 15:7)

Christ and His love enter into the mess we've made of our lives. He forgives us, cleanses us, and gives us right standing with God. From the beginning of time God knew our name and our life story from start to finish. He knows our weaknesses and failings, and He chose to love us. He has called us out of the darkness of bondage to sin into the light of life and liberty—because He chooses to love even those who are unlovable.

Now, in the same way, we are called upon to love our brothers and sisters in Christ. We tend to be unlovable, offensive, and self-centered. But we love and accept each other as we are, and then strengthen each other to grow strong in the faith.

> *Brothers and sisters, do not slander one another.*
> *Anyone who speaks against a brother or sister or judges them speaks*
> *against the law and judges it.*
> (James 4:11)

Sanctified saints will distance themselves from the church grapevine. Gossip is one of the most vicious ways to destroy fellowship in a gathering of faith. Instead of spreading tales, we are to speak with wisdom and teach each other with instructive words.[12] Slanderous chatter is the fruit of self-centered lives, arrogant thinking, and it causes disorder. Rumors taste so good at first, but they create a bitter root that goes down deep in our soul.[13]

But we get clever and cloak our gossip in ways that seem so spiritual. We mutter to a friend, "Pray for Joe, I think he's hitting the bottle again. And his wife looks so depressed. Pray for her too." This kind of judgmental attitude is contrary to the law of love. Christ's love drives us to go stand beside Joe and his wife in their time of need and pray with them rather than talk about them. Disparaging mutterings are opposed to grace and mercy. Slanderous words are an assault against Christ and our neighbor.

> *Love and faithfulness meet together; righteousness and peace kiss each other.*
> (Psalm 85:10)

This is a holy embrace of the covenant between sanctified saints. God's word is powerfully effective for leading us to saving faith. The gift of faith is the means for those who are called to Christ to be justified. We are made right with God in the righteousness of Jesus Christ. Once we are justified, the "work out our salvation" part begins.

This work of sanctification can happen even when someone is alone in their car listening to the radio. God's word has a way of penetrating the highest, thickest walls we build in our hearts, and He breaks in at the most unexpected places. There are times when there are man-made walls around us, and yet they offer no obstacle to God's work of righteousness in us. Aleksandr Solzhenitsyn, Dietrich Bonhoeffer, Corrie ten Boom and many others could testify that the Lord is more than able to accomplish His sanctifying work in those who are locked away. Most Christians have not been privileged to suffer as they did.[14] Instead, God's work of sanctification most often occurs in community.

The Lord's typical means of sanctification is a gathering in Jesus' name where the word is preached, discussed, and tested to prove what is taught. In

---

12. Proverbs 31:26.
13. Proverbs 18:8.
14. Romans 5:3–5.

our assemblies, we are encouraged and strengthened as we see the effect of the righteousness of Jesus Christ at work to sanctify us together in His name.

Each of the verses in this study brought to light one aspect of what it means to be made holy. The words, deeds, and actions of sanctified saints are the effect of the righteousness of Jesus Christ at work in us. They are brought to fruition by the power of the Spirit at work through the Word of creation. God's word is the sword that separates us to righteousness and compels us to deeds of love, faith, service, and self-sacrifice.[15]

> *"For I was hungry and you gave me something to eat,*
> *I was thirsty and you gave me something to drink,*
> *I was a stranger and you invited me in,*
> *I needed clothes and you clothed me,*
> *I was sick and you looked after me,*
> I was in prison and you came to visit me."
> (Matthew 25:35–36)

---

5. Sanctified in Gathering
Q & A

1. How is a Christian sanctified, and why is this so important?

_____
_____
_____

2. What are the "tools" that work sanctification in us?

_____
_____
_____

3. What is our part in sanctification?

_____
_____
_____

4. Describe the fruit of sanctification in a Christian's life.

_____
_____
_____

---

15. Revelation 2:19.

My Journal Notes:

Chapter 6
The Fullness of Christ in Fellowship

Key Scriptures:

- "For in Christ all the fullness of the Deity lives in bodily form, and in Christ you have been brought to fullness. He is the head over every power and authority." (Colossians 2:9–10)

- "So Christ himself gave the apostles, the prophets, the evangelists, the pastors and teachers, to equip his people for works of service, so that the body of Christ may be built up until we all reach unity in the faith and in the knowledge of the Son of God and become mature, attaining to the whole measure of the fullness of Christ." (Ephesians 4:11–13)

The "fullness of Christ" is a beautiful phrase that Paul uses in a letter to the Ephesian church. He also wrote to the Colossians about being brought to fullness in Christ. What does Paul mean by the fullness of Christ, and how are we brought into it? It would take many books to fully describe our Savior's richness, if it's even possible. Words cannot describe the abundance of Christ, but this study points us in the right direction. We will also come to see the obstacles we have set up that keep us from the riches of God's kingdom.

Though none of us will come to a pinnacle of perfection in this life, even so we are called to press forward to receive all Christ ministers to us. To push on doesn't mean that we, by our own effort or in our own strength, work to reach some artificial measure of piety. Instead, we have a way opened to enter into the abundance of the kingdom of heaven. Our Lord Jesus opened the way, and today is the day to enter.[1] We look forward to eternal blessings, but we are called to enter by faith into this abundance now.

At the very moment when Jesus gave up His spirit as He hung on the cross, the veil that shrouded the Holy of Holies was torn open from top to bottom. Before this time only the high priest could enter the Holy of Holies, and then only once a year.[2] Now, in Christ, because the curtain was rent in two, we may enter into God's holy presence. We surrender all of ourselves to Christ in this holy place, and Christ accomplishes His good work in yielded souls.

Let's press on to learn the effects of this miraculous work Jesus accomplishes in our hearts and lives. The following is incomplete, but it's like turning the key for your car—it's a good place to start. We can learn more of what

---
1. Hebrews 3:15.
2. Hebrews 9:7.

He holds out to us in His nail-pierced hands.

In His fullness, we come to know more of the splendor and beauty of His name. We grow to function as parts of His body (the church). We live and walk by faith in the resurrection power of Christ. God's saving grace is manifested to us. The Light of Life lights our pathway. As we press forward, we are given the key to knowledge of our Lord and Savior. Every day of our lives is a search to know wisdom and truth. Godly love is preeminent in our lives and saturates every action, word, and relationship. Christ, the Word, provides direction for our footsteps through the day and night. We come before God, in Christ, with great reverence and awe to bow in His presence and worship at His footstool.[3] With humble hearts and contrite in spirit, we come into the Father's favor.[4] To realize the fullness of Christ, we receive the empowering work of the Spirit of Christ for the ministries of all spiritual gifts given to strengthen the church.

In the fullness of Christ, we are given generous hearts. God's commands are written on our hearts. A willingness to sacrifice on behalf the kingdom of heaven inspires our deeds. True humility is the essence of the words we speak. With a penitent spirit, we come before the throne of grace. We consider others better than ourselves. Our hearts are ready to forgive those who offend or harm us. We live our lives in keeping with repentance. Every day our baptism is fulfilled in us—we have died to sin, and we are raised up in the power of the resurrected Christ. It is in Him that we are brought into peace with our heavenly Father.[5]

It would be natural to think, "this is impossible." But in forgiveness and mercy, we press on toward the goal. Now we will learn about some of the obstacles that keep us from all that our Lord Jesus holds out to us.

One barrier that keeps us from the abundance of Christ is a pervasive individualistic sentiment in American culture. I've heard too many people say, "I love Jesus, I just can't do the church thing." But that's like saying, "I enjoy a sip of cool water when I'm thirsty but don't ever expect me to swallow it." When we give up gathering together in Jesus' name, we have created a recipe for serious spiritual dehydration.

The hitch is that we tend to see ourselves as mavericks, blazing our own trail. When westernized Christians read, "We have gained access by faith into this grace,"[6] we have a mindset that interprets it as, "I have access." While true, our individualism excludes us from one of the greatest blessings of God's

---

3. Psalm 99:5.
4. Isaiah 66:2.
5. Romans 5:1–2.
6. Romans 5:2.

grace, and that is to be a functioning part in a fellowship of Christian faith. It's a good thing to pray in the solitude of our prayer closet, but the power of praying in agreement with a community of faith is awesome beyond comparison. We can worship the Lord with singing as we tend our tomato vines. This song of praise is like the flame of a single candle. But a time of singing in corporate worship is like the mighty blaze of many candles. The flame of one candle might be blown out, but together the candles will reignite each other.

How can a body function if there is only one part or one candle? Christians are not like single-celled amoebas. The path we're on isn't intended to be like, just me and my horse. Christ Jesus, the Head of the church, has made all of us together to be His body—the church. He does not want to accomplish His divine plan without followers serving as His hands and feet. Because of this, Jesus Christ has made His body, the church, with many working parts. And all these various parts work better together.

Paul refers to this community of faith in his epistle to the Colossians. He teaches that our leaders, elders, teachers, presbyters, pastors, and evangelists are a special gift. Their work is to serve, equip, train, build-up, and teach, so that the saints may become unified in faith, brought together as one body in Christ, made complete in the knowledge of God's Son, and grow in grace and knowledge. The fullness of Christ is best accomplished in a gathering of the body of Christ. Our teachers, elders and pastors, who are anointed to minister, help to serve this good purpose.

To fully function under the headship of our High Priest, Jesus Christ, and do our part as the body of Christ, we are called to gather together in Jesus' name. We do not come into the fullness of Christ or the richness of the kingdom of heaven as self-sufficient individuals. As new creations in Christ, we are made part of a whole. Conforming to Christ in His body is the way into the fullness of Christ and the richness of the Gospel.

With boldness we enter into God's holy presence because we come before God in Christ, and in the fullness of Christ. We stand before the Father surrounded by a great cloud of witnesses and a community of faith. We come before the Father with our sins forgiven, washed, and cleansed by the blood of the Lamb. We stand before the Father washed in the waters of holy baptism. We enter into God's holy presence as we gather together at the Lord's Table. And all the goodness of God's kingdom is held out to us in our worship gatherings in Jesus' name. We are brought together in the ministries of our High Priest, Jesus Christ, and together we come into the fullness of Christ.

*I press on toward the goal to win the prize for which God has
called me heavenward in Christ Jesus.*
(Philippians 3:14)

6. The Fullness of Christ in Fellowship
Q & A

1. What obstacles have kept you from knowing the fullness of Christ?
   _____
   _____

2. Why is gathering together an important part of entering into the richness of Christ?
   _____
   _____

My Journal Notes:

Chapter 7
Together We are the Temple of the Holy Spirit

Key Scriptures:
- "Do you not know that your bodies are temples of the Holy Spirit, who is in you, whom you have received from God?" (1 Corinthians 6:19)
- "In him the whole building is joined together and rises to become a holy temple in the Lord." (Ephesians 2:21)

When you visit the Grand Cathedrals, temples, and synagogues built since the Middle Ages, you see architectural marvels constructed with hand-carved quarry stone. Their spires reach to the sky to cast long shadows over the ancient thoroughfares below. The stained glass, icons, and statues of the apostles will overwhelm you with a sense of awe. Most of Europe's basilicas took hundreds of years to construct. They were designed and built by people who worked with deep-felt devotion. Master builders often worked a lifetime, and then passed on the work to others to carry forward. But God does not dwell in these awesome, man-made structures.

In this chapter we'll learn about the temple where the Holy Spirit dwells. When the Scriptures say that our bodies are the temple of the Holy Spirit, does this mean there are many temples, or are we all together as one temple? And what is the human body's function in this temple the Spirit inhabits? We'll learn that our body serves a good purpose, and for that reason we need to keep our body healthy as possible for as long as possible.

In a gathering of faith, together as one in Christ, we are made to be the temple of the Holy Spirit—a holy temple. This place of worship is built with precious, living stones, and it's as if its chambers are inlaid with pure gold. We have a sanctuary built with costly stones and priceless metals, and it's important to keep this temple clean. But how do we do the necessary cleaning?

Who has a part in the building of the temple? Who are the building stones for this haven of worship? We will learn that this temple the Holy Spirit inhabits is built by the power of the Spirit, and not by mortal strength and might.

The Spirit of Christ dwells in our inner being, that is, our spirit. The temporal vessel for our spirit is the body that we feed, exercise, and care for. There is a great benefit in this connection.

And if the Spirit of him who raised Jesus from the dead is living in you, he who raised Christ from the dead will also give life to your mortal bodies because of his Spirit who lives in you.
(Romans 8:9–11)

We must care for and strengthen these bodies so they can do their job as vessels for soul and spirit. Christian's mortal bodies serve the sacred purpose of keeping our feet planted on terra firma until the day we are called home. The Apostle Paul teaches us that our bodies are no longer our own.

You were bought at a price. Therefore honor God with your bodies.
(1 Corinthians 6:20)

This temporal vessel that we shave and shower in the morning belongs to God, it's the temple of the Holy Spirit, and worth taking good care of.

If anyone destroys God's temple, God will destroy that person; for God's temple is sacred, and you together are that temple.
(1 Corinthians 3:17)

We take care of our own body's needs, strengthen our spirit, and serve the well-being of the whole body of Christ. When we care for our earth suits, and grow in grace and knowledge, we do so in agreement with Jesus' High Priestly prayer:

"My prayer is not that you take them out of the world but that you protect them from the evil one. They are not of the world, even as I am not of it."
(John 17:15–16)

Now, in the temple of the Living God, we must put aside all that would hinder, distract, pollute, or destroy this faith-built temple. This is the reason there can be no association between the temple of God and idolatry.

For we are the temple of the living God. As God has said: "I will live with them and walk among them, and I will be their God, and they will be my people."
(2 Corinthians 6:16)

As one in Christ, all Christians together are the temple where the Holy Spirit comes to dwell.[1] The prophet Isaiah made it clear that the place of worship where the Spirit of Christ dwells is not many but one tent to encompass all who are called by His name.

---

1. 1 Corinthians 3:16.

> *"Enlarge the place of your tent, stretch your tent curtains wide, do not hold back;*
> *lengthen your cords, strengthen your stakes."*
> *(Isaiah 54:2)*

We are all made one in Christ. As the church grows, the tent curtains will be stretched wide to welcome all who are drawn to Christ—all who will hear, believe, and obey. But the tent requires a bit of work to keep it clean for the Holy Spirit.

> *For the flesh desires what is contrary to the Spirit, and the Spirit what is*
> *contrary to the flesh. They are in conflict with each other.*
> *(Galatians 5:17)*

Just as brick and mortar require regular cleaning, the temple needs repeated cleansing because sinful flesh leaves a mess to clean up. As a community of believers, we are called to examine ourselves, and confess our sins, weaknesses, and failures. In repentance we will overcome, and God is faithful to cleanse us.

> *This is what the Sovereign Lord, the Holy One of Israel, says:*
> *"In repentance and rest is your salvation."*
> *(Isaiah 30:15)*

King Solomon was commissioned to build the temple of worship in Jerusalem. He inlaid the interior of the temple with pure gold.[2] This offers us an excellent principle with regard to the temple the Holy Spirit indwells. Pure gold! The Holy Spirit does not dwell in a temple built with wood, hay, and stubble—materials that cannot withstand the fire of the Spirit.[3] God's temple, where the Spirit of Jesus dwells, is built upon Christ, who is the foundation stone.[4] The house of worship is raised up on this sure footing with many precious building stones. The Apostle John wrote about overcomers in Christ:

> *The one who is victorious I will make a pillar in the temple of my God.*
> *(Revelation 3:12)*

We are united as one in Christ who is the Chief Cornerstone of the church.[5] Those who overcome in Christ are living stones and pillars in the temple for the glory of Christ who is the Capstone.[6] Everyone in Christ is one precious stone in this temple that encompasses all of us together. God's saints are the jewels of God's kingdom. All of us, as one, are the temple where

---

2. 1 Kings 6:21.
3. 1 Corinthians 3:13.
4. Isaiah 28:16.
5. 1 Peter 2:6–7.
6. Zechariah 4:7.

the Holy Spirit comes to dwell. In his revelatory vision, the Apostle John was shown the Holy City built with precious stones.

And he carried me away in the Spirit to a mountain great and high, and showed me the Holy City, Jerusalem, coming down out of heaven from God. It shone with the glory of God, and its brilliance was like that of a very precious jewel, like a jasper, clear as crystal.
(Revelation 21:10–11)

All those who are called by His name are the precious jewels of the kingdom of heaven. We are the bride adorned with the Bridegroom's ornaments prepared for His coming.[7] When we allow God's word to broaden our perspective, we will see that all the saints together are the temple of the Spirit of Christ. We are raised up and made one in Christ. This is the temple the Lord inhabits—a tabernacle that inspired the Psalmists to sing:

Within your temple, O God, we meditate on your unfailing love.
(Psalm 48:9)

It's important to remember that those who oppose Christ have no part in the temple. The prophet Ezra made this truth clear to Bishlam, Mithredath, Tabeel and associates, who volunteered to help build.

"Let us help you build because, like you, we seek your God and have been sacrificing to him since the time of Esarhaddon king of Assyria, who brought us here."
(Ezra 4:2)

They got a quick and unified answer.

"You have no part with us in building a temple to our God. We alone will build it for the Lord, the God of Israel, as King Cyrus, the king of Persia, commanded us."
(Ezra 4:3)

For those who are given the desire to come to Christ, we stretch the tent curtains wide to welcome them. And yet, we must give no part in the work to those who oppose Christ. Shouldn't Ezra and Zerubbabel have welcomed all the help they could get? Sometimes it's best to keep the enemy close to know what they're up to. But in rejecting the help, they made clear that God's temple was to be constructed with precious stones alone. The house of worship would be built:

"Not by might nor by power, but by my Spirit," says the Lord Almighty.
(Zechariah 4:6)

---

7. Revelation 21:2.

That is, not by human might and power, but in the power of the Spirit. In the same way, the Holy Spirit dwells in a temple made from the living stones—people who confess:

I have been crucified with Christ and I no longer live, but Christ lives in me.
(Galatians 2:20)

The Holy Spirit doesn't dwell in man-made structures, no matter how grand and glorious they may be. A cathedral's stained-glass windows illustrate stories of Jesus' birth, ministry, death, and resurrection to help us learn. The tall steeples point to the cross of Jesus Christ, and yet, the Spirit of Christ does not dwell in hand-cut stone or brick and mortar structures. Instead, the Spirit of Jesus dwells in our inner being, i.e. our spirit. The reborn spirit of man is housed in a temporal vessel—our earth-bound body. Because of this it's important to take care of ourselves and keep our body as healthy as we can to serve its good purpose until the day we are called home to wait for our body to be glorified.

Together we are the temple of the Holy Spirit, a sanctuary of worship. Each of us is like a precious, living building stone that makes up a part of the whole. This temple has a solid foundation, as Paul wrote to the Ephesian church:

Consequently, you are no longer foreigners and strangers, but fellow citizens with God's people and also members of his household, built on the foundation of the apostles and prophets, with Christ Jesus himself as the chief cornerstone.
(Ephesians 2:19–20)

To keep the temple clean, we must recognize our sin and sinfulness, confess our sin, repent of our sin, and receive the cleansing of forgiveness. This is a cleansing from all unrighteousness that is accomplished by blood of the Lamb of God. The word and the Spirit of Jesus convict us of our sin and show us our need of Christ. The Apostle John wrote to the church of Sardis:

Yet you have a few people in Sardis who have not soiled their clothes. They will walk with me, dressed in white, for they are worthy.
(Revelation 3:4)

Part of keeping things pure and clean is that no one who opposes Christ will be given any share in the temple. We welcome all who are called to seek our Lord and Savior, and yet those who rebel against Him and stand in opposition to Him will be given no part in it. This is a temple that is not built by means of mortal strength and power but by the power of the Spirit.

Let us come together as one in Christ, in the unity and power of the Holy Spirit, to be the precious, living building stones for the temple of worship. Together in the Sanctuary, we will sing the praises of God of our salvation.

May the stones cry out as one voice of joyful praise in the temple, a gathering of God's people.

7. Together we are the Temple of the Holy Spirit
Q & A

1. Describe the building stones for the temple of the Holy Spirit.
   ___
   ___
   ___

2. Regarding this temple, what is the role of our physical body?
   ___
   ___
   ___

3. How is the temple kept clean?
   ___
   ___
   ___

My Journal Notes:

Chapter 8
Pillars Upon the Rock

Key Scriptures:

- "If I am delayed, you will know how people ought to conduct themselves in God's household, which is the church of the living God, the pillar and foundation of the truth." (1 Timothy 3:15)
- "When the earth and all its people quake, it is I who hold its pillars firm." (Psalm 75:3)
- "On this rock I will build my church, and the gates of Hades will not overcome it." (Matthew 16:18)

We live in a world that provides no place to anchor our lives. Every change of the wind affects our social norms, politics, values, ethics, and even our language. These bumps in the road tend to throw us off the safe course we have charted for ourselves. Graduations, weddings, divorces, and funerals change our family life. The kids grow up and leave us with an empty nest. After we hit the mandatory age of retirement, we're left with a blank appointment calendar to stare at every morning.

The meanings of words change with the winds of time, and a common word becomes an insult. Food we once enjoyed as wholesome is declared a hazard to our health. Laws become obsolete and even ridiculous. The way we communicate shifts like sand under our feet.

Beyond any doubt, we live with constant disruption. The strongholds of this world are determined to undermine and overthrow the church our Lord Jesus Christ has established. Jesus implied that many storms would assault the church. He declared that, "In this world you will have trouble."[1]

Indeed, there is trouble all around us, but even pandemics and hateful violence cannot destroy those who will gather in Jesus' name. Jesus assured us that the gates of hell could not, and would not, prevail against the church.[2] The kingdom of darkness will not triumph even when the buildings where we gather are torched. This is because we have the confident assurance of knowing Jesus our Rock. Jesus Christ is the unshakeable and enduring foundation for the pillars of the church, and we will not be forever thrown down. In this study, we'll come to know Christ as the Rock upon whom the pillars of the church are firmly established. We'll identify the true pillars that support those

---
1. John 16:33.
2. Matthew 16:18.

who are brought together in Christ.

Every soul on earth has a deep-seated need for certainty—a rock-solid place to anchor. Every child has an inherent need for well-established values and boundaries. The current epidemic of depression in our country proves that foundational values are critical for our sense of well-being. Without a secure spiritual Rock, people are faced with a wide path in front of them that leads to a dead end.

The chaotic history of the ancient nation of Israel gives us a prime example of the effect of eroding foundations. The book of Judges offers a record of their sin and resulting chaos, and it ends with a scathing reproof of their spiritual decay. God Almighty made them into a nation and served as their king, but they rejected Him. Jehovah God gave them His Law as a secure pathway for their lives, their family, and for the nation, but they scorned the ancient paths.[3]

> *In those days Israel had no king; everyone did as they saw fit.*
> (Judges 21:25)

We tend to walk down the same wide, destructive pathway[4] in danger of rejecting the Rock upon whom the church is built. It's a frightening thought that history repeats itself. Terms like "Christless Christianity"[5] express this alarming reality.

Yet, we find great hope in repentance. Confession, and turning from our own pathway, brings us back into fellowship with Christ. Once again, we will find a mooring for our lives, and in Him we find the very core, purpose, and focus of our worship gatherings.

> *Lead me to the rock that is higher than I, for you have been my refuge,*
> *a strong tower against the enemy.*
> (Psalm 61:2–3)

We find great promise in Christ Jesus in whom we anchor. In Him we come to the foundation of truth where the Gospel is revealed. At first, the Good News may seem like a mystery. But then, when we hear the promises of saving grace, the seed of faith is planted in us. We are compelled by the truth to press forward in obedience, we are baptized and made to be one with Christ and His body, the church. Now our feet are set upon our Rock in whom we find security. Our lives and our eternal destiny are secure—rock sol-

---

3. Jeremiah 18:15.
4. Jeremiah 18:15.
5. Michael Horton, Christless Christianity: The Alternative Gospel of the American Church (Michigan: Baker Books, 2008).

id because of Him. In Christ we find the certainty we need, and we're rescued from the foolishness of sinking sands.

"But everyone who hears these words of mine and does not put them into practice is like a foolish man who built his house on sand."
(Matthew 7:26)

The church may be shaken, burned out, driven out, or shouted out, but this is only for a moment, because we are victorious in Christ. The gates of hell will not prevail against us. Picture a community of faith as they stand in front of the burned-out building where they once gathered. They stare with blank faces, arm in arm, while tears stream down their ashen faces. A charred concrete foundation is all that's left of the library, classrooms, sanctuary, kitchen, and the fellowship hall. The smoke of fire-scorched debris and ashes assaults their senses. Through their tears the crowd breaks out in spontaneous song.

> In Christ alone my hope is found
> He is my light, my strength, my song
> This Cornerstone, this solid ground
> Firm through the fiercest drought and storm
> What heights of love, what depths of peace
> When fears are stilled, when strivings cease
> My Comforter, my All in All
> Here in the love of Christ I stand[6]

This gathering of believers, though shaken, has something solid to stand on that's better than bricks and mortar. They have a great hope because they are victors in Christ, the cornerstone.[7] In Him they are made to stand firm on the word of the Lord. They are the true pillars of the church. All who overcome in Christ are the supports, like columns that serve as the sinews of the church. They stand firm to cheer on all those who serve in ministries of help, missionaries, prayer warriors, administrators, teachers, elders, deacons, and pastors. Worship, service and ministry in our gatherings are all strengthened because of the supporting pillars. Evangelists who preach the Gospel are strengthened by those who stand with them. Families and communities of faith are refreshed in their presence. They are faithful to intercede and act on behalf of the weak and the helpless. The poor among them find an ear to listen and hands that open to them in their time of need.

---

6. Natalie Grant, vocalist, "In Christ Alone," by Keith Getty and Stuart Townend, track 12 on Relentless, Curb Records, 2008.
7. Isaiah 28:16.

This is not to say we must earn our way to become a stalwart of the church. We are made pillars by means of grace. No matter our age, status, or energy level, the pillars of the church are those who are made victorious in Christ. For the structure to be strong, there must not be some pillars who do all the work and sandbags who hold down the seats in our gatherings. The people in the front row and those who sit in the last row are all called to strengthen the church.[8] This is the very reason we are called to admonish and encourage each other. When one of us is weak, the whole structure suffers. Christ builds His church one victorious soul at a time, and together He makes us the temple of the Holy Spirit.

The one who is victorious I will make a pillar in the temple of my God. Never again will they leave it. I will write on them the name of my God and the name of the city of my God, the new Jerusalem, which is coming down out of heaven from my God; and I will also write on them my new name.
(Revelation 3:12)

Many churches teach that elements of worship like confession, absolution, Bible study, meditation, fasting, prayer, as well as other traditions and practices are the pillars of the church. But this is like saying the grapes support the vine that produced them. True and real worship in our gatherings is lifted up and supported by those who have gained the victory in Jesus Christ. God's desire is to dwell in the hearts of His people, not in bricks and mortar.[9] The people of His pasture are the true pillars, the living stones of the temple.

You also, like living stones, are being built into a spiritual house to be a holy priesthood, offering spiritual sacrifices acceptable to God through Jesus Christ.
(1 Peter 2:5)

Everything that can be shaken will be shaken. The words of the prophet Amos make clear what can be shaken. The pillars of the temple are set over the thresholds that are set upon the foundation. The capitals of the temple pillars are of stone, decorated with pomegranates,[10] as if capped with His love. When the capitals are struck, the pillars will be stressed, the thresholds will shake, but the foundation will hold firm.[11]

I saw the Lord standing by the altar, and he said: "Strike the tops of the pillars so that the thresholds shake."
(Amos 9:1)

---

8. Ephesians 4:16.
9. Ezekiel 11:19–20.
10. Song of Songs 7:12.
11. Isaiah 54: 11–12.

It takes victorious people of faith to serve as pillars. In an uncertain, guaranteed-to-change world, we find a solid Rock where we can anchor our lives—Christ, who is the head of the church. A structure that teeters on a lone pillar will not stand. God's truth is established where two or more redeemed souls gather. Our Lord God builds with many towers of strength who are brought together to make the church strong.

We are the temple of the Holy Spirit, the church of the first-born in Christ. We are all called to serve as supporting pillars for our worship gatherings. There should not be those who are looked on as weak pillars, crumbling supports, cracked columns, sandbags, or useless rubble. We must all come together as precious stones to lift up the church to strengthen our worship, service, and ministries for all who will come. Now, we have come to know Christ, the Rock in whom we anchor our lives. We can see His work of grace that molds us and shapes all those who are victors in Christ to be strong pillars of the church.

Truly he is my rock and my salvation;
he is my fortress, I will never be shaken.
(Psalm 62:2)

8. Pillars upon the Rock
Q & A

1. Describe the foundation for the pillars of the church.

2. What are the consequences of rejecting the Rock upon whom the church is built?

3. Who are the pillars of the church?

My Journal Notes:

Chapter 9
Together We Stand in God's Council

Key Scriptures:

- "Praise the Lord. I will extol the Lord with all my heart in the council of the upright and in the assembly." (Psalm 111:1)

- "But which of them has stood in the council of the Lord to see or to hear his word? Who has listened and heard his word?" (Jeremiah 23:18)

- "My hand will be against the prophets who see false visions and utter lying divinations. They will not belong to the council of my people or be listed in the records of Israel, nor will they enter the land of Israel. Then you will know that I am the Sovereign Lord." (Ezekiel 13:9)

God's council has many dimensions, like the facets of a diamond. To see the various aspects, first picture a well-cushioned couch where soulmates get together. Then think about a group wrapped in familiar conversation around a coffee table. Consider a circle of friends who are bonded together because they share a confidence. Now look to the cross and see those who come on bended knee with one heart and mind to seek the Lord Almighty.

In God's council we hear wise words, as if breathed out for all who will hear. In this assembly there are teachers, elders, prophets, servants, and helpers—the "priesthood of all believers."[1] God's council is all-hands-on-deck to minister, serve, and advance the Gospel.

In God's council He is held in great awe and greatly feared.[2] The Lord Almighty is exalted in this sacred meeting. And the most awesome aspect of the council: It's a place where God's word is carried out. The very oracles of God are spoken and ministered to those in the congregation, and these life-giving words spread from there like fire.

It's a challenge to distinguish between God's church and His council—as difficult as discerning between soul and spirit. Church and council fit together like hand and glove. All the Scriptures about God's council lead us to see the church as a wheel, and God's council like fire that bursts out from it. It's where the proverbial rubber hits the road.

These word pictures give us a sense of God's council. In this study, we'll explore the significance of God's council. We'll ask the question: Does the Lord Almighty, Creator of all heaven and earth need a council to give Him

---
1. 1 Peter 2:5.
2. Psalm 89:7.

counsel? And we'll come to understand the power and effect of this holy assembly.

Join us now as we recline on our cushioned couch and find comfort in God's holy presence. The conversation in this council is relaxed and cordial because it's a group of friends who share a trust and a bond of Christian love. The people who serve in this conclave have been molded and shaped by the Potter[3] to be made useful in service of the kingdom.

With the above examples, we begin to get a sense the Hebrew word from Psalm 111:1: çôwd. God's council is a resting place.[4] It's a peaceful habitation, a joining of hearts for true intimate affections. When the layers are peeled away, we come to rest on Jesus, so close that we can hear His heartbeat. In this holy conclave, God's word is breathed out in the power of the Spirit of Christ to fill the sanctuary with sweet-smelling aromas. This is the garden of God where the branches of the vine flourish, prosper, and bear good fruit. In the planting of the Lord, we come to know God by His name that reveals more and more of His nature, like the opening of rose petals.

Consider the beautiful flower bud that we offer to our loved one. Its petals, when pulled back one at a time, reveal the sweet fragrance of the flower and finally the heart of the rose. This is an illustration of our heavenly Father's nature to reveal himself. What He reveals must first be a mystery—hidden—not obvious to the natural mind. Indeed, the Lord God is shrouded in darkness.[5] For this reason, the Gospel is a mystery to be revealed, and the kingdom of heaven must be opened to us.

David, who became king of Israel, was called a man after God's own heart[6] because he opened the rose petals, so to speak, to search for the heart of God. In his quest, he came into God's council—close to God's heart. The sons of Korah sang of this passionate search to know the Lord in this psalm.

> *As the deer pants for streams of water, so my soul pants for you, my God.*
> *My soul thirsts for God, for the living God. When can I go and meet with God?*
> (Psalm 42:1–2)

How do we pull back the layers that bring us to the center where we stand in God's council, lean upon Him, and hear His heartbeat? David wrote a Psalm to show us the way.

---

3. Isaiah 64:8.
4. Psalm 132:8.
5. Psalm 18:11.
6. Acts 13:22.

Your righteousness is like the highest mountains, your justice like the great deep. You, Lord, preserve both people and animals. How priceless is your unfailing love, O God! People take refuge in the shadow of your wings. They feast on the abundance of your house; you give them drink from your river of delights. For with you is the fountain of life; in your light we see light.
(Psalm 36:6–9)

First, David exalted the Lord of righteousness. He sang out praise to God who preserves both mankind and the animals. He chanted a psalm of God's unfailing love. He took refuge in the shadow of God's wings. He feasted on the abundance of the Lord's Table. He drank from the river of God's delights. The psalmist immersed himself in the fountain of life, and then walked in the light to see light.

We too can pull back the rose petals one by one. Let's look at how we can do this. Seek first God's kingdom. Pursue His righteousness.[7] Search for the one your heart loves.[8] Take refuge in the Lord.[9] Drink deep of the Living Water.[10] Search to know the holy Scriptures.[11] Look for the Lord with all your heart and soul.[12] Meditate on God's word.[13] Seek first His kingdom and His righteousness. Sow seeds of righteousness in the world around you.[14] Ask, so that you may come close to the heart of God.[15] There are many more petals of the rose bud to pull back, so take each petal, one at a time, and come into God's council—nearer to the very heart of God.

We are all beckoned to stand in God's council. This isn't only for super Christians and dynamic leaders. All who come to saving faith may seek and come to stand as one in God's holy presence as part of this blessed assembly. In this council we find communion with people of faith. With hearts and minds in concert the chaos of the world is left behind, and we come into a well-ordered assembly, gently guided by those who lead us. In council, near to the heart of God, we are strengthened to accomplish the work God prepared in advance for us to do.

Those who walk shoulder to shoulder with the ungodly may not come close to God's heart. Continuing in rebellion while walking a broad pathway to satisfy the desires of the flesh disqualifies a person from this blessed fellowship. Joining in with mockers will block the gates to this holy commission.

---

7. Matthew 6:33.
8. Song of Songs 3:2.
9. Psalm 36:7.
10. John 4:14.
11. 2 Timothy 3:15.
12. Deuteronomy 4:29.
13. Psalm 119:15.
14. Hosea 10:12.
15. Luke 11:9.

Hearts with divided loyalties cannot enter here. This is not an intellectual pursuit, but a mindful love of God helps to light the way. Being close to God's heart is not earned, but effort is encouraged.

What does God's council look like? What are the characteristics of such a conclave? It's like being awash in the depths of the river of righteousness that flows from the throne of God. The Spirit of Christ speaks and inspires every word that is proclaimed. Our hands become the hands of Christ to reach and touch those whom the Lord God is touching. Every word taught and preached is confirmed, tested, and weighed by truth and light from the holy Scriptures. God's people, in council, judge according to all righteousness.[16]

Those who join in this gathering are of noble character. They are eager to receive the message and test it to be sure the truth is taught.[17] In God's council, those who hear God's word examine it using the unchanging counsel of God as revealed in the Bible.

> *The counsel of the Lord stands forever,*
> *the plans of his heart to all generations.*
> (Psalm 33:11)

Does God who created all that exists in this universe need counsel from His council? Does the Lord Almighty need our advice, ideas, or our thoughts? In his letter to the Corinthian church, Paul made this issue clear. We are to have the mind of Christ, which is to have a heart submitted to God.

> *"Who has known the mind of the Lord so as to instruct him?"*
> *But we have the mind of Christ.*
> (1 Corinthians 2:16)

While the Lord has no need of our counsel, He wants us to come into covenant with Him to accomplish the work of the kingdom of heaven. God's people, the church, receive the Gospel message with gladness. God's council is where the Good News goes into action—to work, serve, minister, and lead the congregation in praise and worship before the Lord.

God's council is plugged into the power source. This is where we press forward to know God's heart, purpose, and plans. In this place the desire of God's heart becomes the desire of our heart. God's purpose becomes our purpose. Partners in God's council are like the vintners who serve the Father who is the vine dresser. These workers sow seeds of righteousness and serve as laborers in a plentiful harvest.[18] They are prepared, armored up with God's

---

16. 1 Corinthians 6:1–3.
17. Acts 17:11.
18. Matthew 9:35–38.

armor, and made ready for the day of battle.[19] With God's word as a sword they are like Eleazar who struck down his enemies "till his hand grew tired and froze to the sword."[20] This band of servants is like David's mighty men who joined with the Lord in battle, not by human might and strength, but in the power and strength of the Spirit.

God's council is a place for the bride who waits with great expectation. Her eyes strain to see the Promised One. She has oil for her lamp in expectation of the Bridegroom's coming. Jesus, lover of our souls, speaks of His bride with great affection.

> *Awake, north wind! Rise up, south wind!*
> *Blow on my garden and spread its fragrance all around.*
> (Song of Songs 4:16 NLT)

Knock and the door will be opened. As you cross the threshold into God's council, a sweet fragrance like that of a rose bud will greet you. We come together in Jesus' holy name to hear God's counsel. This is a place of comfort, a gathering of shared confidence, and a base for action. The council's job is to accomplish the work of the kingdom in the power of the Spirit of Christ. In this sacred assembly we are servants, laborers, and warriors. His bride, in council, is like an "orchard of pomegranates with choice fruits, with henna and nard."[21]

God's council serves to proclaim the Gospel message. To accomplish this good work we are anointed, gifted, and empowered with the oil of the Spirit of Jesus. We are like beautiful feet on the mountain to bring Good News, proclaim peace, announce good tidings, and proclaim God's saving grace.[22]

In our gatherings we shout out in joyful worship, serve and minister, stand in God's council, and exalt the Lord God of our salvation. This is for the priesthood of all believers who seek first the Kingdom of God. This is for a faithful congregation that holds to the truths of a simple and beautiful Gospel. In this counsel, all that is preached and taught is tested and proved with God's word as a plumb line.[23]

The church may be likened to a wheel and God's council like flames from the wheel. As we press in to know the heart of God, His words become like fire in our mouths[24] to do the work of the wheel, i.e. the church. This is the power, the effect, the sweet comfort, and the blessings that come from gather-

---

19. Psalm 110:3.
20. 2 Samuel 23:10.
21. Song of Songs 4:13.
22. Isaiah 52:7.
23. Amos 7:7.
24. Jeremiah 5:14.

ing close to God's heart as servants in this holy council.

Pull back the petals of the rose, one at a time, and come near to the heart of God to stand in His council.

---

9. Together we Stand in God's Council
Q & A

1. What are the characteristics of God's council?

2. Does the Almighty need counsel from His council?

3. Who may be a part of this holy assembly?

My Journal Notes:

Part II
Gather All Your Children to You

"Lift up your eyes and look around;
all your children gather and come to you.
As surely as I live," declares the Lord,
"you will wear them all as ornaments;
you will put them on, like a bride."
(Isaiah 49:18)

Chapter 10
It Takes a Gathering to Serve

Key Scriptures:

- "You, my brothers and sisters, were called to be free. But do not use your freedom to indulge the flesh; rather, serve one another humbly in love." (Galatians 5:13)

- "Jesus called them together and said, 'You know that the rulers of the Gentiles lord it over them, and their high officials exercise authority over them. Not so with you. Instead, whoever wants to become great among you must be your servant, and whoever wants to be first must be your slave—just as the Son of Man did not come to be served, but to serve, and to give his life as a ransom for many.'" (Matthew 20:25–28)

There is a love story each of us writes with the words we speak and the life we live. The best love stories start with Christ because He loved us first. Then our written narrative continues year after year with reflections on the steps we take in response to Christ's love. Our life sketches will often include accounts of Christ's abundant forgiveness that inspire us to love even more. Our deeds, words, and actions recorded in journals offer proof of love-inspired affection toward our Lord and Savior. This devoted relationship is a story about fruitfulness by means of His saving graces. And then, our last chapter before forever is about love-inspired deeds that will be commended on the day of the Lord.

What will you write in your personal love story? Will it be about your steps into the joys of serving, like a flower girl at a wedding who spreads blossoms of sunshine for the bride's pathway?

As servants in the kingdom of heaven, we throw off those things that are only of value in a fallen world. There is no need to struggle and climb the corporate ladder that leads to nowhere. Gaining authority over others has no eternal value. When examined by the plumb line of Scripture, we will find that this corrupted sphere is upside-down. But there is a higher realm that is true to plumb.

David and his mighty men, who gathered in the wilderness, will show us how bonds of love inspired them to bold acts of service. A woman caught up in sin will illustrate how abundant forgiveness inspired her extravagant acts of loving service. We'll learn from Jesus' example. As He pressed on to Jerusalem and the cross, He stepped away from dinner to wash the disciples' feet as if he were a household servant.

We'll come to see how important it is to gather where hearts become inclined to serve in submission to Christ. Without a gathering of faith, how can there be any opportunity to serve? Jesus came as Immanuel, God with us, and He came to serve. Jesus instructed His followers, then and now, to "Follow me." We are called to step in His footsteps as servants of the Most High God.

I have yet to meet anyone whose life goal was to become a servant. There is no public University or Christian school that offers a major in servanthood. And yet, in the kingdom of heaven that is our objective. As He walked among us, Jesus showed us the heart and soul of serving. He came as Immanuel, a humble servant, born in a stable and placed in a cow's trough. His dad figure here on earth was a simple carpenter.

Think of the people in your life who are unreserved in the way they serve others. In any gathering, whether around a dinner table, at the fire pit in the backyard roasting marshmallows, or at Thanksgiving and Christmas gatherings, they delight in serving whatever need they can find. They will offer you more sweet potatoes and pumpkin pie because you enjoyed the first helping so much. These are the most delightful and happy people you will ever know. They spread sunshine. They are like springtime and flowers. If you come to a get-together feeling glum, their brightness drives the blues away.

Jesus gathered His disciples saying, "Follow me." And for over three years in Jesus University, He taught His disciples to serve. Then, when Jesus knew the hour had come, He pressed on toward the cross with the disciples at His side. One evening as they gathered to share a meal, Jesus showed them the full extent of His love.[1] He threw off His garment, got down on His knees, and washed the disciples' feet as if He were the household servant.

But instead of serving, our natural inclination is to establish chains of command—unless we're the bottom link, of course. We scratch and claw our way to climb up the corporate ladder. We work our way to the top of the organizational pyramid, gather people around to serve our needs, make others answer to us, and we work hard to gain authority over the worker types. But if we gain the world, what do we have that will last, let alone for eternity?[2] When we give account of our lives to the Lord on that great day before His throne of judgment, we will not boast about how many people have served us. Rather, our hearts will be weighed based on how we helped others. Did we serve with the mind and heart of Christ?

---

1. John 13:1.
2. Mark 8:36.

Jesus' servant heart shows us that our human default mode isn't suitable for the work of His kingdom. As Jesus sent out the disciples, He told them to proclaim:

> *"The kingdom of heaven has come near."*
> (Matthew 10:7)

In the realm of heaven's economy, we find that our human values are backwards. The domain Jesus' disciples proclaimed is one in which human weakness reveals the Lord as mighty. In heaven's dominion, the Lord God is our sovereign, and in Christ His bondservants find freedom. In Christ's realm, the humbled are given the riches of the kingdom of heaven, the meek inherit the earth, the persecuted find themselves blessed, and through the ashes of our lives we find the beauty of Christ. Where God reigns, our greatest human effort offers little of long-term value. In heaven's kingdom, our human inabilities reveal God's infinite abilities. In the same way, Christ's love toward us finds its greatest fulfillment in deeds of humble service. Even simple acts toward those who seem insignificant are of great significance.

> *"And if anyone gives even a cup of cold water to one of these little ones who is my disciple, truly I tell you, that person will certainly not lose their reward."*
> *(Matthew 10:42)*

Christ Jesus' love at work in us is revealed in acts of service. Jesus' passion is fulfilled in us as we set aside our own ambitions to serve others. Our ministries are the fruit, effect, and proof of the extent of our love of our Lord and God. To take up the mantle of a bondservant, we must put off Earth's glitter and glamor and enter God's kingdom of glory and majesty. As we step into Christ's realm, His love blossoms in us to bear good fruit, and this is the fulfillment and proof of His grace, mercy, and loving kindness at work in us. To serve the cause of Christ is our life purpose. Servanthood is our position in Christ. We are called to be servant priests.

> *To him who loves us and has freed us from our sins by his blood, and has made us to be a kingdom and priests* **to serve** *his God and Father–*
> *to him be glory and power for ever and ever! Amen.*
> (Revelation 1:5–6; emphasis added)

Christ's love and forgiveness compels us to give of ourselves with love as our motive. When a woman who had been snared in sin brought a jar of expensive perfume to anoint Jesus, the host protested. The woman wept at Jesus' feet and wiped them with her hair. What a scene it must have been as the room filled with a fragrance of love. Jesus responded to the host's objections with a parable about two debtors, one who owed an immense sum and another who owed a little. The lesson was clear.

> *"Therefore, I tell you, her many sins have been forgiven—as her great love has shown. But whoever has been forgiven little loves little."*
> (Luke 7:47)

When we see a person who is zealous for Christ and the Gospel, remember that it's likely they have received abundant forgiveness, and with great effect. The loving forgiveness of Christ washes through them and then floods out to soak their neighbors with acts of abundant love. Many worship gatherings have sung out this truth: "Love so amazing, so divine, demands my soul, my life, my all."[3]

The story of David in the wilderness offers a beautiful illustration of the thrust of gathering together in Jesus' name. Like David and his band of men, in the bonds of fellowship, our burdens are lifted through forgiveness, and we are inspired to acts of loving service. Our love-driven deeds reveal that Christ's love is fulfilled in our hearts. The Apostle John shows us a perfect example of this. He wrote about Jesus' act of washing the disciples' feet. He made an incredible statement about Jesus' purpose.

> *Having loved his own who were in the world, he now showed them the full extent of his love.*
> (John 13:1 NIV)

It's important to understand the Greek word that most translators interpret as: loved them to the "end." The Greek word , télos, could just as well, in context, be translated: "loved them without limit." Jesus' teaching prepared them for His death, burial, resurrection, and ascension to the right hand of the Father. He taught them to love and serve so they would follow in His footsteps to complete the work of the Great Commission.

Try to imagine a gathering of God's people who love their brothers and sisters in Christ without limit. What would happen if our worship time overflowed with the infinite love of Christ? How would limitless love cause those to serve who are sent out in Jesus' name? How would the world around us be different if boundless love ruled the day? Humanistic world views are upside down because, in fact, the greatest love is demonstrated and proven with deeds carried out in submission to Christ.

How would we live if we knew our days on earth were short? Would we get out our bucket list and credit card and live it up? "Eat, drink, and be

---

3. Isaac Watts, author, "When I Survey the Wondrous Cross," Hymns and Spiritual Songs, 1707.

merry" sounds like a good plan to many people who know that their life will soon come to an end. There's a better way. Those who gather family and friends around them to offer final words of blessing will never be forgotten. Gifts of wisdom from a life well-lived are a timeless bequest. This kind of servant's heart is the effect of the righteousness of Jesus Christ at work in us and through us. Look to Jesus as our example. He knew the time was near as He walked on toward Jerusalem, prepared to offer up His life for the sins of all humankind. In this moment, He served to wash the disciples' dusty feet as one of His final acts of love.

Keep in mind that it takes a gathering to serve. If Jesus walked alone on His way to Jerusalem, or if He dined alone as He pressed on toward the cross, there would only be two feet to wash and no one to teach. Hermits don't have anyone to serve but themselves. Loners can't help anyone but the person they see in the mirror. How can you be of service if you're the only one there? It's not possible! Come, join in the joyous procession so we may worship and serve together.

But thanks be to God, who always leads us as captives in Christ's triumphal procession and uses us to spread the aroma of the knowledge of him everywhere.
(2 Corinthians 2:14)

In Christ, we are compelled to serve others with boldness. Jesus knew that the Father had put all things under his power, and that he had come from God and was returning to God.
(John 13:3)

He knew His position before God Almighty, and He washed the feet of the disciples. He was confident in God's purpose and plan, and He bent His knees to serve. Jesus knew He was the only Son of the Most High God, and He showed His followers the heart of a servant. When we know beyond doubt that we are sons and daughters of the Lord who reigns on high, our hearts will be compelled to help our neighbor. When we know we are blood-bought saints, we're inspired to lend a hand. The cleansing effect of forgiveness compels us to acts of loving kindness. When our calling is sure—and we know the Spirit of Christ has anointed, gifted, and empowered us—we can bend our knees to meet a brother or sister's need with confident assurance because the One who reigns on high is our Heavenly Father.

We are born into an upside-down world and taught in backwards classrooms. This environment will never prepare us for service and ministries in Christ. The system teaches us how important it is to get ahead in life. We push ourselves to get that degree so we can shatter glass ceilings. We work long and hard to get ahead in life, no matter who we leave behind in the dust.

But in Christ we enter a kingdom that is right-side up. In our gatherings in Jesus' name, we are called to a work of service that is neither above nor beneath us. Thousand-dollar fashions or bargain basement sweat suits don't make us who we are in Christ. Before Jesus washed the disciples' feet, He threw off His outer garments. This act teaches us that it's important to remove things that would hinder us and then bow down as a servant to serve. In Christ, we are exalted to serve above our low earthly standing, and we are humbled to work beneath our position in this life.

Jesus offers us a living example of serving our neighbors. He began His ministry on earth with a call to: "Follow me." As the resurrected Christ He said to His disciples once more, "Follow me." With the mind of Christ, and the heart of our Lord Jesus, we are called to follow in His footsteps—the imprints of a loving servant.

Will you join a gathering in Jesus' name to inspire your love story? The story of a servant.

---

10. It Takes a Gathering to Serve
Q & A

1. What will you write as your life's personal love story?
___
___
___

2. How is it that forgiveness inspires us to acts of service?
___
___
___

3. What natural inclinations do we need to guard against?
___
___
___

4. Describe Jesus' "love without limit."
___
___
___

My Journal Notes:

Chapter 11
Serving Before our High Priest

Key Scriptures:

- "Let the message of Christ dwell among you richly as you teach and admonish one another with all wisdom through psalms, hymns, and songs from the Spirit, singing to God with gratitude in your hearts." (Colossians 3:16)
- "Carry each other's burdens, and in this way you will fulfill the law of Christ." (Galatians 6:2)
- "Submit to one another out of reverence for Christ." (Ephesians 5:21)

Many of Jesus' followers have wondered: "Who am I in Christ? What is my part in the kingdom of heaven?" Too often we stumble around trying to find our niche in a Christian gathering. This chapter is prepared to help us answer those questions. It's an invitation to jump into the flow of God's river of righteousness to carry out our calling in Christ with the heart of a servant.

We will learn where this mighty river begins and how it floods the earth with God's glory. This study teaches us to fulfill our God-given role in the work of the Great Commission. One important tenet we will learn, as we are prepared for ministry, is being cleansed to serve. We will discover how mercy, offered and received in like manner, performs a crucial role in "one-another" kinds of gatherings.

Each of us is created special and unique. There is a work prepared for us, custom made to fit us. Whether simple or complex, gifted ministries are given to strengthen the body of Christ. When we all serve according to our appointed mission, the body of Christ becomes like a well-oiled instrument in the hands of Jesus, our High Priest.

Christian gatherings ought to be like snowmelt that trickles into brooks to feed crystal-clear mountain lakes. The lakes teem with life, and then the water streams into rivers with pools and rapids flowing down to the foothills and out to a vast ocean.

In the same way, when we gather to receive of the ministries of our High Priest, Jesus Christ, the blessings pour out in increasing measure. This is the awesome power of the ministries of our High Priest. The good things given to us are like an artesian spring that pours out to make the meadows blossom.

When the Spirit of Christ ministers in our gatherings, we in turn are empowered to minister and serve those who assemble with us. And then, as we are blessed by others, we are stirred up to go out to minister and serve those we rub elbows with every day. The river's current is continuous, powerful, and cannot be stopped up for long. This is the power and effect of the river Ezekiel prophesied. The water from the temple started as a trickle, like the flow from Jesus' pierced side, soon to become an uncrossable river.

> *And the water was trickling from the south side. As the man went eastward with a measuring line in his hand, he measured off a thousand cubits and then led me through water that was ankle-deep. He measured off another thousand cubits and led me through water that was knee-deep. He measured off another thousand and led me through water that was up to the waist. He measured off another thousand, but now it was a river that I could not cross, because the water had risen and was deep enough to swim in–a river that no one could cross.*
> (Ezekiel 47:2–5)

This miraculous river is a picture of a victorious church swept along in the river of God's righteousness. It's a river that delights the city of God.[1] The service and ministries of Jesus Christ our High Priest become a mighty torrent, and the river gets deeper and wider as the church flourishes. God shows Himself holy through His people, and the great mystery of the saving grace is revealed more and more. We must press on to pursue Gospel mysteries that the human mind finds difficult to perceive. This ever-increasing, powerful river sweeps us along until we will become "like the roar of rushing waters."[2]

The blood and water that gushed from Jesus' pierced side increases in a flood of service and ministries of the saints. The Gospel bursts forth like a torrent to cover the earth.

> *For the earth will be filled with the knowledge of the glory of the Lord as the waters cover the sea.*
> (Habakkuk 2:14)

For all who thirst, living water floods out to satisfy. God's purpose is clear. Like a shepherd, He gathers the sheep of His pasture to His heart. The power of the blood of Christ cleanses us so that we may be useful servants to accomplish the work appointed to us. By the work of the cross, Jesus, the righteous servant, affects righteousness in us. The power and effect of this work of righteousness compels us to serve and minister.

---

1. Psalm 46:4.
2. Revelation 19:6.

> *How much more, then, will the blood of Christ, who through the eternal Spirit offered himself unblemished to God, cleanse our consciences from acts that lead to death, so that we may serve the living God!*
> (Hebrews 9:14)

His cleansing is complete. Christ's work to purify us is better than Adam and Eve's fig-leaf moment in an attempt to cover their sins.[3] Being washed in the blood of Christ is greater than the Old Covenant where sins were covered by the blood of sacrificial animals. For Christians today, we are made clean from the inside out. Jesus does the deepest kind of cleaning in our lives. We come boldly before the throne of grace, made pure and holy in Christ. He goes to the depth of our consciousness to wash us clean.

> *Because of Christ and our faith in him, we can now come boldly and confidently into God's presence.*
> (Ephesians 3:12 NLT)

As holy servants we enter into God's presence where we are forgiven, cleansed, and anointed to be sent out to do the work of the kingdom of heaven. Indeed, we are cleansed to serve.

The power of this river of righteousness is awesome. Listen to Jesus' eternal words:

> *On the last and greatest day of the festival, Jesus stood and said in a loud voice, "Let anyone who is thirsty come to me and drink. Whoever believes in me, as Scripture has said, rivers of living water will flow from within them." By this he meant the Spirit, whom those who believed in him were later to receive. Up to that time the Spirit had not been given, since Jesus had not yet been glorified.*
> (John 7:37–39)

Step into the powerful stream of living water and serve as a fountain that pours from the threshold—that is Christ. The Scriptures give us another beautiful analogy, encouraging us to let our roots grow deep beside the streams of living water to become like trees that bear fruit in season.[4]

Producing imperishable fruit is impossible apart from the anointing, gifting, and empowering work of the Spirit of Christ who is the True Vine. By means of the Living Water we are made to be trees of righteousness, to always be fruitful. We are cleansed and healed for a purpose. Our work is to open our mouth to speak the word, to let the Living Water pour out. We proclaim the Good News to the poor, declare freedom in Christ, blaze out with the light of the Christ to the spiritually blind, set free those who are bound in the

---

3. Genesis 3:7.
4. Psalm 1:3.

chains of sin, strengthen the weak, bind up the wounds of the brokenhearted, and bring good cheer as a medicine to those who suffer.

Consider the ministries of grace. The beauty of the work of grace is that we can't make it happen. Yes, we are called to acts of grace, but apart from the Spirit of Jesus, the work is impossible. Our part is to live and speak the message of the Gospel in a loving, caring, and tactful manner, so that the holy Scripture can do its work on the hearts and souls of those who will hear. To prepare, we saturate ourselves with God's word so that it becomes woven into our heart and soul. Then the Holy Spirit will bring these life-giving words to mind for the right person in their moment of need. There is great joy to see the word and the Spirit work through us and change a person's life forever.

All who are spiritually thirsty and starved are welcome to step into this river of righteousness by faith and be flooded with Christ Jesus in holy baptism. The Bread of Life and Living Water will satisfy parched lives. Hungry, thirsty, and without means of our own, we are drawn to this powerful stream by the word and the Spirit. With our thirst satisfied, joy overwhelms us. Filled with wonder, we take this living water to those around us, to proclaim in Jesus' name:

Come, all you who are thirsty, come to the waters; and you who have no money, come, buy and eat! Come, buy wine and milk without money and without cost.
(Isaiah 55:1)

By the power of the Spirit we will speak out Jesus' words:

But whoever drinks the water I give them will never thirst. Indeed, the water I give them will become in them a spring of water welling up to eternal life.
(John 4:14)

By the anointing of the Spirit of Christ we bring our friends and family to Jesus who declared:

"I am the bread of life. Whoever comes to me will never go hungry, and whoever believes in me will never be thirsty."
(John 6:35)

This is the power of the increasing currents of God's river of righteousness. We are called to serve the weak, to strengthen them. With our mouths we speak words of grace. We are the very hands of Christ Jesus to those who are weak. We open our hands to those who are burdened in poverty. Our hearts reach out to our neighbors who are caught up in sin's darkness. The prophet Isaiah recorded what God spoke to His people, words that we are called to proclaim.

Strengthen the feeble hands, steady the knees that give way; say to those with fearful hearts, "Be strong, do not fear; your God will come, he will come with vengeance; with divine retribution he will come to save you." Then will the eyes of the blind be opened and the ears of the deaf unstopped. Then will the lame leap like a deer, and the mute tongue shout for joy. Water will gush forth in the wilderness and streams in the desert. The burning sand will become a pool, the thirsty ground bubbling springs.
(Isaiah 35:3–7)

The love of Christ floods through the saints like a river in the springtime.

May the Lord make your love increase and overflow for each other and for everyone else, just as ours does for you.
(1 Thessalonians 3:12)

The Spirit of Christ ministers healing to those gathered, and we likewise serve as His hands extended to heal, according to the spiritual gift given to us as the Spirit wills.

*Is anyone among you sick? Let them call the elders of the church to pray over them and anoint them with oil in the name of the Lord. And the prayer offered in faith will make the sick person well; the Lord will raise them up.
If they have sinned, they will be forgiven.*
(James 5:14–15)

We become prepared as ambassadors of the Most High God as we apply this chapter to our lives. The purpose of this instruction is to compel us to jump into the great river of righteousness to be swept along in the cause of Christ. With this knowledge solidified in our hearts and minds, we begin to fulfill our purpose in God's kingdom. This chapter's lesson joins us together with the Apostle Paul who encouraged the church to act and serve by means of faith.

With this in mind, we constantly pray for you, that our God may make you worthy of his calling, and that by his power he may bring to fruition your every desire for goodness and your every deed prompted by faith.
(2 Thessalonians 1:11)

The Scriptures illuminated in this chapter reveal the miraculous river that began as a trickle and turns into a mighty flow that covers the earth with words of saving grace and peace. We have learned that Jesus ministers the Gospel so that we may be His voice to speak out the Good News to all who will hear. We can see how vital it is to receive from the ministries of our High Priest, Jesus, so that we may be anointed to serve. Our ministries to one another in our gatherings prepare us to be sent out to spread the light of Christ and to flood our surroundings with Living Waters.

Whether modest or monumental, our spiritual gifts serve to strengthen the church. My prayer is that each of us will receive and stir up our God-given spiritual gifts and enter the increasing flow of the river of righteousness. In Jesus' own words:

> *"Whoever believes in me, as Scripture has said,*
> *rivers of living water will flow from within them."*
> (John 7:38)

---

11. Serving Before our High Priest
Q & A

1. What does it mean to minister and serve before Christ Jesus our High Priest?

2. How is the trickle that turns into a mighty river likened to the church?

3. What does it mean to be God's ambassador?

4. How does Jesus minister the Gospel today?

My Journal Notes:

Chapter 12
Spiritual Gifts Imparted

Key Scriptures:

- "I long to see you so that I may impart to you some spiritual gift to make you strong—that is, that you and I may be mutually encouraged by each other's faith." (Romans 1:11–12)

- "For this reason I remind you to fan into flame the gift of God, which is in you through the laying on of my hands." (2 Timothy 1:6)

- "Do not neglect your gift, which was given you through prophecy when the body of elders laid their hands on you." (1 Timothy 4:14)

- "Each of you should use whatever gift you have received to serve others, as faithful stewards of God's grace in its various forms." (1 Peter 4:10)

This study focuses on the abundant graces extended to those who gather in Jesus' name. God's gifts to His people are lavished upon us as workers who build the church with living stones. Our High Priest, Jesus Christ, pours out various spiritual gifts upon His people who gather so they may be strengthened, encouraged, healed, and restored—all for the glory of His holy name. A leader's heart desire ought to be for people to receive spiritual gifts, and then serve, empowered in their gift.

To teach us, the Apostle Paul shows us a spiritual gift being imparted to Timothy by means of an inspired prophetic declaration and laying his hands on him. The gift imparted to Timothy—and the gifts imparted to us today—fortifies the church and enables the saints to do what would otherwise be impossible. In the ministries of spiritual gifts, God is glorified, and lives are changed for all eternity.

Spiritual gifts are most often imparted before witnesses to encourage those who gather to receive and serve in accord with their calling. Jesus' command, "Follow me,"[1] is a call for every disciple to serve and minister, and we are each given unique tasks to accomplish. The special gifts entrusted to us in a gathering go with us as we are sent out to minister and serve in the community. Every one of Christ's disciples is one of a kind and the work we do in our spiritual gift is custom made for us to accomplish.

The Apostle Paul's heart burst with a longing for God's people who were placed in his care. This desire proved his love for them and his zeal for the Gospel. He wanted the disciples to be strong in the Lord, so he imparted

---
1. John 21:19.

spiritual gifts to them as the Holy Spirit desired. The great benefit of these gifts, for them and for us, is to be strengthened and encouraged in saving faith and for the work of the Great Commission. Christ Jesus continues to minister His grace today through shepherds who serve as Paul served. It's important to note that Paul didn't encourage them to discover their spiritual gift. He didn't give a written test to find their personal strengths. He didn't give them a personality exam or ask them about special abilities on their jobs. He didn't do this because these kinds of tests and questions are designed to help us discover the natural or common gifts we were born with. Unlike common talents, the gifts of the Holy Spirit are for the work of the Great Commission. Each of us is given a task so the work of the church will be completed.

Paul imparted spiritual gifts to the believers so they could do what would otherwise be impossible on their own. These powerful abilities are not presumed[2] but given as the Spirit wills in agreement with God's purpose and plan. Our High Priest, Jesus Christ, knows the needs of each local gathering of believers, and the Spirit of Jesus imparts spiritual gifts to meet the need in a community of faith. Note that Paul imparted the gifts prophetically as he laid his hands on Timothy. In a very real sense, he acted in the authority of Christ, by the command of our Lord Jesus. God spoke through him by means of the gift of prophecy, and his hands served as if they were Jesus' hands to impart the spiritual gift. He ministered under the authority of Christ; he submitted to Jesus our High Priest. He spoke what Jesus was speaking, and he placed his hands on Timothy to minister in Jesus' name.

The point is clear. Spiritual gifts are given to strengthen those who gather together as one in the faith. They are conferred upon all who will receive them for the greater good of the church. Gifts of the Spirit empower each of us to do the job God designed for us even before time began.

> *For we are God's handiwork, created in Christ Jesus to do good works,*
> *which God prepared in advance for us to do.*
> (Ephesians 2:10)

Paul didn't take Timothy aside for the gift to be imparted but ministered while surrounded by witnesses in a public gathering. It was typical for Paul, the elders, and the people to spend time in prayer and fasting to know the heart of God before they conveyed spiritual gifts. Even today, what is intended for the good of all is imparted in the presence of all who are gathered together. Paul ministered in this way to make the whole gathering ready to press on toward the goal.

---

2. James 3:1.

> *Therefore, preparing your minds for action, and being sober-minded,*
> *set your hope fully on the grace that will be brought to you at the*
> *revelation of Jesus Christ.*
> (1 Peter 1:13 ESV)

We, like Timothy, have a call to serve. God knew us and every moment of our lives before time began, and He designated a special work for each to accomplish for the good of all. Spiritual gifts are most often imparted during an assembly of Jesus' disciples because they are intended to strengthen and encourage the whole community of believers.

> *Each of you should use whatever gift you have received to serve others,*
> *as faithful stewards of God's grace in its various forms*
> (1 Peter 4:10)

Are spiritual gifts only for a congregation in times of worship? When we are sent out from a worship gathering, are we suddenly separated from the ministry gifts of the Spirit? Not at all. When Jesus brings us together, all those who will come are woven together like a fabric, various threads knitted together in a bond of community. We are never separated from Christ and the power of fellowship as we are sent out. It's as if everyone from the gathering is still with us, including their prayers and encouragement. The bond of community fellowship will continue to strengthen us. Our High Priest prepares us for battle in the congregation. He arms us with the word of God as a sword and protects us with the breastplate of righteousness. We are given faith as a shield as we are sent out. It's in an assembly that our feet are "fitted with the readiness of the gospel of peace."[3] Jesus sent out his disciples in teams of two. His Spirit went with them in power and authority to make it a threesome. Jesus told the disciples:

> *"I have given you authority to trample on snakes and scorpions and to overcome all the*
> *power of the enemy; nothing will harm you."*
> (Luke 10:19)

In the same way, when we are sent out from a worship gathering, we go with a beautiful declaration:

> *"How beautiful are the feet of those who bring good news!"*
> (Romans 10:15)

The power and authority of our High Priest, Jesus Christ and His body, the church, are the inspiration for those who are sent. All authority is by Jesus' command and this authority goes with all who are sent.

---
3. Ephesians 6:15.

> *"Therefore go and make disciples of all nations, baptizing them in the name of the Father and of the Son and of the Holy Spirit, and teaching them to obey everything I have commanded you. And surely I am with you always, to the very end of the age."*
> (Matthew 28:19–20)

The ministries of spiritual gifts are awesome to witness. In fact, spiritual gifts are one of three witnesses that give testimony of Christ dwelling in us and we in Christ.[4] The Spirit, the water, and the blood testify that Jesus is the Christ, Son of the living God. The Spirit who is Giver of all good gifts, the waters of holy baptism and the cup of the Lord's Table, gives testimony of the Spirit of Christ who indwells us.

With regard to spiritual gifts, consider that every disciple of Jesus is unique. Our souls are as different as fingerprints. All Christians are called to serve as priests, and we are given unique gifts that are a perfect fit. Spiritual gifts are given as the Spirit wills so we may accomplish the various tasks assigned to us.

> *Each of you should use whatever gift you have received to serve others, as faithful stewards of God's grace in its various forms.*
> (1 Peter 4:10)

In our gatherings, we are equipped and empowered to go tell of His saving grace. By means of grace, the Spirit of Jesus sends unique and special souls to minister and serve with spiritual gifts the Holy Spirit has imparted. When we are sent as ambassadors of Christ, our Lord Jesus puts us together with people that might only hear the Gospel because our heart and soul connect with their heart and soul in a unique and special way.

All this is possible because we are anointed, gifted, and empowered by the Spirit of Jesus, who serves in our gatherings as High Priest. Can you picture the Good Shepherd gathering His flock, to hold His precious lambs in arms of love, close to His heart? He tends his flock like a shepherd:

> *He gathers the lambs in his arms and carries them close to his heart; he gently leads those that have young.*
> (Isaiah 40:11)

With the heart and mind of Christ, the shepherds in our gatherings desire all of Jesus' disciples to receive spiritual gifts, and in this way strengthen the whole body of Christ, His church.

We witnessed the Apostle Paul impart a spiritual gift to Timothy by means of prophetic words and laying his hands on him. This served to em-

---

4. 1 John 5:6–10.

power Timothy for his part in the work of the Great Commission. Our High Priest, as Head of the church, ordains shepherds to serve the church. They are blessed with the heart of mind of Christ, to serve as He served. With the heart of a shepherd, an elder, pastor, or presbyter will impart spiritual gifts to those in his care to strengthen all who gather in Jesus' name.

The work of the church and the Great Commission are an impossible work for man to accomplish by human strength alone. Temporal gifts are inadequate for an eternal work. But in Christ, and by means of the gifts given by the Spirit of Christ, the work we are given becomes mission possible—all for the glory of God. The whole church, the priesthood of all believers, are called to serve according to their spiritual gift. The gifts of the Spirit are intended to strengthen the community of believers as we are sent out to minister and serve. We serve as the light of Christ to drive back the darkness of a fallen world by means of the Spirit's power and strength and by the authority of Jesus' command.

All Christians who gather and witness spiritual gifts as they are imparted are encouraged to receive the Spirit's gifts so they too may minister and serve for the good of all. What is imparted in community serves to bind us together like a tightly woven fabric. Bound together, we are empowered to fulfill our calling for the cause of Christ. Each of us will accomplish a unique and special work that would be impossible apart from the gifts of grace given as the Spirit wills. All this is accomplished by means of the power of Christ, the Head of the church, and the Spirit of Christ who gathers with us and sends us out in the authority of His holy name. We follow in Jesus' footsteps to minister and serve, empowered to serve by the Holy Spirit:

> *"Not by might nor by power, but by my Spirit," says the Lord Almighty.*
> *(Zechariah 4:6)*

12. Spiritual Gifts Imparted
Q & A

1. What is God's purpose in giving spiritual gifts to the church?

2. How do our gatherings benefit from the ministries of spiritual gifts?

3. Why are spiritual gifts typically imparted in a gathering?

4. How do spiritual gifts make the impossible work of the kingdom possible?

My Journal Notes:

Chapter 13
Strengthened for Victory

Key Scriptures:

- "And I tell you that you are Peter, and on this rock I will build my church, and the gates of Hades will not overcome it." (Matthew 16:18)

- "I am writing to you, fathers, because you know him who is from the beginning. I am writing to you, young men, because you have overcome the evil one." (1 John 2:13–14)

- "You, dear children, are from God and have overcome them, because the one who is in you is greater than the one who is in the world." (1 John 4:4)

- "In fact, this is love for God: to keep his commands. And his commands are not burdensome, for everyone born of God overcomes the world. This is the victory that has overcome the world, even our faith." (1 John 5:3–4)

- "To him who overcomes I will grant to sit with Me on My throne, as I also overcame and sat down with My Father on His throne." (Revelation 3:21 NKJV)

In the Apostle John's Revelation of Jesus Christ, he wrote, "To the one who is victorious."[1] He is speaking of Jesus who has overcome the world and defeated the power of sin and death once and for all time. And now, our Lord Jesus Christ brings us into His victory. Together we are triumphant with Him and made overcomers.

In this chapter's study we'll learn why our own weak and futile efforts have worn us out. We are called to turn from our own means, repent of our self-reliance, and receive the anointing, gifting, and empowering work of the Spirit of Christ. We will see the value of being united in strength to overcome. This chapter teaches how to become conquerors as we gather together in Jesus' holy name. In His strength we become victorious in the eternal work of the Great Commission. This is not a job for mavericks, but for a host of saints raised up in Jesus' name.

To be sure, victory in Christ is not about social justice. Marching arm in arm together and singing protest songs isn't the most effective way to defeat the evils of this world. But for those who are victorious in Christ one notable side effect is social justice. By the work of the cross, Jesus Christ has overcome the world on our behalf, and all who are in Christ are overcomers with Him.

---
1. Revelation 3:21.

When we are triumphant in Christ, the world's oppression and violence are defeated. Efforts toward social justice are a worthy cause, but we must not treat the symptoms and ignore the disease. There is a better way, and the results are eternal.

We live in an upside-down world where might is right, money is power, and the winner takes all. We don't view it as backwards because what we see with our eyes and touch with our hands is often our only reality. But this physical world we live in is finite, while the kingdom of heaven is infinite. The eternal is the greatest reality because it provides a rock-solid footing, while this natural earth is like shifting sand. And it's in the realm of God's kingdom that we come into victory.

Because it's hard to perceive what is real and forever, we make Bible heroes like Samson into a muscle-bound superhero. We think of David's mighty men as if they had some kind of superhuman strength. We illustrate the whole armor of God with physically powerful warriors clad with Roman armor. But this is not the way of God's kingdom. Human vigor is not the means of victory. Jesus shows us heaven's path to victory.

> *Rejoice greatly, Daughter Zion! Shout, Daughter Jerusalem! See, your king comes to you, righteous and victorious, lowly and riding on a donkey, on a colt, the foal of a donkey.*
> (Zechariah 9:9)

The prophet Zechariah got it right. A forever kind of victory isn't won by the strongest armies. Humility and meekness are the means for victory. Our best weapon in the battle against temptation is the word of God, and not man-made armaments. We must be honest with ourselves. On our best day, with our minds clear and sharp, wearing our finest clothes, and our hair just right, we cannot accomplish the work God has prepared for us to do.

> *And he is not served by human hands, as if he needed anything. Rather, he himself gives everyone life and breath and everything else.*
> (Acts 17:25)

Jesus commands us to do the work of the Great Commission, but it cannot be fulfilled by means of human strength, ingenuity, or abilities. This is not a mission that can be completed even by the greatest strength and ability on earth. The message of the Gospel is not proclaimed by means of great oratory or eloquent words. The power and truth of the Gospel are not conveyed by persuasive arguments. The highest worship, service, and ministry is not accomplished by the strength of human hands but by holy hands. The world's greatest minds could never carry out the task to spread the Good News to every tribe, nation, and language group. Again, Zechariah emphasizes this truth.

> *"Not by might nor by power, but by my Spirit," says the Lord Almighty.*
> (Zechariah 4:6)

This is important! We must give up the struggle that wears us out. Think about it. We get burned out because we try to accomplish an impossible mission in our own strength. We have been given a workload that's unbearable apart from the good gifts, power, and work of the Spirit of Christ. The heroes of our faith were not great people in the eyes of the world. Noah built an ark where there was no place to float a boat. And then, he served to save a remnant of God's creation from the flood. Moses didn't deliver God's people with a mighty army. He was given a simple shepherd's staff. John the Baptizer announced the coming Messiah in a remote place, by a muddy river, not with a parade and a band of trumpeters. Instead of a muscle-bound superhero type, God sent a babe in a manger. Jesus didn't ride victorious into Jerusalem as a conquering king in a golden chariot pulled by a team of six white horses. He rode into the city on a donkey's colt, as the Prince of Peace.

God's victory is revealed in weak vessels. This is a frequent theme in our study, but the extra emphasis is important. We must not think like Greeks who have their all-powerful, almighty super gods. They are false gods created by the imaginations of men. We need to put aside a Greek mindset and serve with the mind of Christ—with the attitude of Christ. Knowing our human limitations and weaknesses, we ought to come before a holy God with nothing of ourselves to offer. We are called to be victorious like Abraham who acknowledged that his body was well past child-bearing years and believed God would still give him a son. With this mindset, we present ourselves as moldable, teachable, and useful vessels for the work of the kingdom. When we recognize our human weaknesses, we become useful vessels for the work of the kingdom. Acknowledging our inability is part of preparing ourselves to accomplish all that Jesus commanded as He ascended to the right hand of the Father. Jesus didn't leave us in a helpless state. He sent the Holy Spirit so that we may overcome. We present ourselves as weak vessels to be made victors by means of the anointing oil of the Spirit.

How is a great work accomplished with weak and fallible instruments? How do we overcome our human limitations to gain the victory? "We gave it our best effort and put on a good show, but the job overwhelmed us." Where do we go to find this power of the Spirit that enables us to do the impossible? Take heart because we have a great hope. Jesus not only commanded the work, but He provides a way.

Typically, a community of faith is the place where God's people are empowered to minister and serve. When we gather, we are armored up for the battle. We are taught how to war against all that stands against us. We are strengthened with the prayers of the saints for the work assigned to us. When we come before the Lord as one in Jesus' name, we are shielded against the firebrands from the enemy of our souls. We rise up victorious, "and mighty is the army that obeys his command."[2]

In our gatherings, we hear truth and righteousness taught. We are strengthened to obey the Good News message. In our assemblies, we are built up to live victorious over everyday temptations. Our human weaknesses are turned into spiritual strengths as we gather together, admonish each other, encourage our brothers and sisters, and learn to obey the Gospel of Jesus Christ.

We gain the victory, and like a mighty army that rallies around their banner, we have cause to lift up triumphant refrains to the heavens. In the power of the Spirit of Christ we are prepared and empowered to accomplish what Jesus commanded. Each one is gifted as the Spirit wills, so that we may do a work of eternal value that God prepared for us before time began.

Many obstacles are thrown in our way to keep us from our calling in Christ, and together in Christ we overcome what might hinder us. A Christian's life is one of warfare against Satan's temptations, attraction of sin, distractions of the world, and desires of the flesh. The chaos of the world seeks to drag us down. Because of this, we need to be strengthened to stand firm in the light of Christ so we may fulfill the call of the Gospel. It isn't enough to win a battle or two and then rest on our laurels. We must "fight the good fight" until we finally overcome the chains that hold us down. We march on, fight on, and persevere to the end, and together we will join in the final great victory celebration.

To the victors is the promise that they may partake of the Tree of Life, which is Christ. We are made to be part of a holy nation, a holy people for God's good purpose.

> *But you are a chosen people, a royal priesthood, a holy nation,*
> *God's special possession, that you may declare the praises of him*
> *who called you out of darkness into his wonderful light.*
> (1 Peter 2:9)

---

2. Joel 2:11.

Together we overcome by the blood of the Lamb of God who takes away the sin of the world. The next day John saw Jesus coming toward him and said:

> *"Look, the Lamb of God, who takes away the sin of the world!"*
> (John 1:29)

We come as one in Jesus' name to overcome the world's temptations, distractions, ambushes, and obstacles so that we may fulfill our calling in the power and strength of the Spirit of Christ. We will gather as victors like the tribes of Israel after they crossed the Red Sea, and then watched as the armies of Pharaoh were destroyed.

> *Then Moses and the Israelites sang this song to the Lord: "I will sing to the Lord, for he is highly exalted. Both horse and driver he has hurled into the sea."*
> (Exodus 15:1)

We have tried to do the work of the church our own way for too long, and we're burned out. We feel defeated, and we're ready to throw in the towel. The work ahead of us seems insurmountable, and we're ready to give it up, exhausted. But there is a great hope, and this hope shines bright in the light of repentance. We must turn away from self-reliance because we are called to minister, serve, and worship in the power and strength of the Spirit of Jesus. The kingdom of heaven is contrary to this natural world we see with our eyes. In God's kingdom, we are like powerless sheep, but God's power is manifested in us and through us as the Good Shepherd gathers us into His sheepfold.

The anointing and strength we need for the task of the Great Commission is found where we gather in Jesus' name because He is present with us. It is here that the Holy Spirit begins to work through us as a community, each one ministering the word of God to strengthen the brothers and sisters in Christ. In our gatherings, good gifts are imparted by means of laying on of hands and prophetic words are offered to confirm the gifts.[3] In our assemblies, we are armored up and strengthened to gain the victory, even against the gates of hell. Together in Jesus' name we are cleansed to serve. The Apostle Paul wrote in his letter:

> *Those who cleanse themselves from the latter will be instruments for special purposes, made holy, useful to the Master and prepared to do any good work.*
> (2 Timothy 2:21)

As one in Christ we will accomplish this impossible work. To go forward we must give up our own efforts and repent of our self-reliance. With contrite hearts, we come before the Lord and find Him faithful to forgive us and

---

3. 1 Timothy 4:14.

cleanse us of all unrighteousness. He is more than able to accomplish all that He has purposed and planned in His church. Our Lord Jesus gathers us together where we gain the victory and are made overcomers in Christ for His good and eternal purpose.

You, dear children, are from God and have overcome them,
because the one who is in you is greater than the one who is in the world.
(1 John 4:4)

---

13. Strengthened for Victory
Q & A

1. What are the "side-effects" of being victorious in Christ?

2. What is the means of, and the source of, our victory?

3. Give some examples of weak Bible characters who were victorious in the power of the Spirit.

4. What is the promise to all those who are victorious in Christ?

My Journal Notes:

Chapter 14
Prepared to Serve

Key Scriptures:

- "So Christ himself gave the apostles, the prophets, the evangelists, the pastors and teachers, to equip his people for works of service, so that the body of Christ may be built up until we all reach unity in the faith and in the knowledge of the Son of God and become mature, attaining to the whole measure of the fullness of Christ." (Ephesians 4:11–13)

- "After this the Lord appointed seventy-two others and sent them two by two ahead of him to every town and place where he was about to go. He told them, 'The harvest is plentiful, but the workers are few. Ask the Lord of the harvest, therefore, to send out workers into his harvest field. Go! I am sending you out like lambs among wolves.'" (Luke 10:1–3)

A lot of preparation goes into getting ready for that first breath our baby will take. And then, life marches on until we finally breathe our last breath. Mom and Dad prepared for our birth by getting the nursery ready. Dad prepared himself by checking the map for the fastest route to the hospital. Grandma and grandpa bought little onesies with "Nana's boy" or "Papa's girl" printed on the front to help them get ready. Life is all about preparation, and it is seldom done solo.

In this study, we'll learn why it's important to get prepared for ministry and service in a community of Christian faith. And finally, we'll come to see the great joy of sending someone out who has been proven and prepared for works of service in our local gatherings.

A young man who was about to be paroled from prison informed me that he made big plans for his release day. The minute they unlocked the gate he was going back, on his own, to a place where he would preach and convert them to the right path. I prayed for him because I knew that, alone, he was way too vulnerable. A greater challenge than his lone ministry was that, in prison he had no opportunity to prepare, learn, grow in faith, and serve as a working part in a church to gain strength and test his spiritual gifts.

We are not meant to minister and serve as a lone pillar of strength. In the same way, it isn't good to train in isolation. Jesus gathered the disciples around Him to teach and prepare them, and then sent them out in groups of two. Paul got prepared in the local churches, and years later teamed up with Barnabus, Aquilla, and Priscilla, and they ministered side by side as apostles and prophets. James and John stood at Peter's side to strengthen each other to lead the church.

Before we partner up in answer to God's call, it's necessary to get prepared. This is best accomplished in a local assembly. The twelve disciples attended Jesus University for three and a half years to prepare them for ministry. They trained with the greatest Teacher and learned from each other's mistakes. Jesus used Peter's impetuous statements to teach truth to His followers. He made use of James and John's selfish ambitions to teach all the disciples about humble servanthood.[1] He used the trick questions of the Pharisees to instruct in the way of the kingdom of heaven. Today, the best preparation still happens in gatherings and classrooms where new Christians are taught, tested, and tried before they are given greater responsibilities. Paul applied this principle to the deacons who were called to serve the church.

> *They must first be tested; and then if there is nothing against them,*
> *let them serve as deacons.*
> (1 Timothy 3:10)

It's important that servants prove faithful with small responsibilities before they take up a greater mantle of service in our gatherings. They must first show they are trustworthy in a few things before they are entrusted with greater responsibility.[2] It helps us to prepare by rubbing elbows with other Christians because they work like sandpaper to smooth off our rough points and hone our flaws. The Apostle Paul cautions against rushing to fill a position in the church because it can get us caught up in the web of another person's sin.

> *Do not be hasty in the laying on of hands,*
> *and do not share in the sins of others. Keep yourself pure.*
> (1 Timothy 5:22)

The heroes of our faith were prepared in unique ways, and often in community. God prepared Joseph to be "in charge" over Egypt by serving his fellow prisoners. Samuel, judge and prophet of Israel, started to prepare when he was still a child. He grew up in the company of priests and was mentored by Eli, the priest at Shiloh. David prepared to lead Israel as king by spending many years hiding in the wilderness with his band of mighty men. The Apostle Paul spent fourteen years establishing local gatherings and then served in the Gentile churches as God prepared him for his missionary journeys.[3]

---

1. Matthew 20:20–28.
2. Matthew 25:23.
3. Galatians 2:1.

Today, those who prepare to serve as pastors are often required to work in a local church before they graduate and fulfill their call. Preparation for service, whether at a university, by mentoring, or by hands-on experience involves us with other people. The gifting and empowering work of the Holy Spirit that is necessary for effective ministry typically occurs in a gathering of faith. To prepare children for a life of faith and service, parents, grandparents, uncles and aunts teach them the simple disciplines of the Christian walk.

The point is clear. In preparation for works of service and ministry, we submit ourselves in a community of faith. It's as if everyone comes together to train and equip us for the work prepared in advance for us to accomplish.[4] We are mentored, molded, shaped up, tested, trained, taught, and gifted in a community of faith.

Whether our calling is to serve as church planter, prophetic ministry, missionary, evangelist, pastor, teacher, administrator, or in ministries of help, we must first submit ourselves in community and be equipped to serve. If our ministry is to serve people from the fellowship's kitchen, we must first prepare and be equipped in a community of faith. Before someone is blessed with the task of teaching our children, they must be tested and trained in our assemblies through the preaching of the word and by imparting the spiritual gift of teaching to them.

One of the greatest celebrations for a Christian assembly is to lay hands on a well-prepared servant, anoint them with oil, and then appoint them to minister and fulfill God's call. Everyone in the gathering plays an integral part in their teaching and training, and they can see the fruit of their faithful efforts. Then, when they are sent out or chosen to serve in the local church, it's like the spreading of tree branches that grow out to bear more good fruit.

The person appointed to serve, whether in a local gathering or sent out to minister, is first tested and prepared in a community of faith. They grow and mature as they are fed on God's word in home Bible studies and in gatherings for worship. They are gifted and empowered by the Spirit in a worship assembly. Then they are anointed and sent as servants. This is one of the abundant joys for a growing and thriving church and a sure sign of the power of the Word at work in our gatherings.

> *Enlarge the place of your tent, stretch your tent curtains wide,*
> *do not hold back; lengthen your cords, strengthen your stakes.*
> (Isaiah 54:2)

---

4. Ephesians 2:10.

14. Prepared to Serve
Q & A

1. How does gathering together prepare us to serve?

2. Give some examples from the Bible of people who were prepared and tested before they began to serve in their calling.

3. Why is submission in a community of Christian faith an important part of preparation to serve?

4. What is a sure sign of a growing and thriving local assembly?

My Journal Notes:

PART III
His Spirit Will Gather Them

Look in the scroll of the Lord and read:
None of these will be missing,
not one will lack her mate.
For it is his mouth that has given the order,
and his Spirit will gather them together.
(Isaiah 34:16)

Chapter 15
Fellowship in Gathering

Key Scriptures:

- "They devoted themselves to the apostles' teaching and to fellowship, to the breaking of bread and to prayer. Everyone was filled with awe at the many wonders and signs performed by the apostles. All the believers were together and had everything in common. They sold property and possessions to give to anyone who had need. Every day they continued to meet together in the temple courts. They broke bread in their homes and ate together with glad and sincere hearts, praising God and enjoying the favor of all the people. And the Lord added to their number daily those who were being saved." (Acts 2:42–47)

- "Therefore if you have any encouragement from being united with Christ, if any comfort from his love, if any common sharing in the Spirit, if any tenderness and compassion, then make my joy complete by being like-minded, having the same love, being one in spirit and of one mind." (Philippians 2:1–2)

The fellowship of a gathering in Jesus' name is a dynamic that affects every part of our lives. It changes the way we live and work. It even makes us better neighbors. When we are joined together in Christ, He transforms our hearts and restores our souls. Our new nature gives us a desire to become part of a joyous assembly. We offer the warmth of hearth and home for others to enter into warm-hearted Christian fellowship. This sweet communion radiates to encompass everything around it. Together, in Jesus' name, we enter into the affections and the afflictions of the Bridegroom, that is, Christ the Head of the church. This kind of gathering has lasting power as sure as the rising of the sun and its setting:

> *It rises at one end of the heavens and makes its circuit to the other;*
> *nothing is deprived of its warmth.*
> (Psalm 19:6)

This chapter's key Scriptures portray an attitude of heart that we would do well to reignite in our day. Luke didn't record history in the book of Acts as a legal paradigm for the modern-day church. Instead, he shows us an attitude of heart that nurtured their unwavering faith and fellowship. But because the believers gave way to their human natures they began to regress. The Apostle John wrote to the church in Ephesus to warn them not to abandon the Rock on whom they were established.

> *Consider how far you have fallen! Repent and do the things you did at first. If you do not repent, I will come to you and remove your lampstand from its place*
> (Revelation 2:5)

In this study, we'll look at the early church to see how much we've changed. Warnings against acts and attitudes that are harmful to fellowship are an important part of this topic. We'll come to know how Christ's presence is evident in our fellowship gatherings. This chapter teaches us to hold fast to the joy of sweet fellowship in Christ and let go of our self-centered ambitions that destroy order in our fellowships. We'll wrap up this study with a call to return to the zeal of our first love to strengthen our fellowship of faith.

The godly acts of the first Christians reflected their profound devotion to Christ. The servant attitude of the converts in Jerusalem reflected enthusiasm for their Lord and Savior. They were like kids with a new ball, like calves let out to pasture in springtime, and like newlyweds learning to live together. They were recklessly in love with Jesus and devoted themselves to serve their new brothers and sisters in Christ. The first Christians were wildly generous, hungry to learn, longed for fellowship, prayed together constantly, and looked forward to the next get-together in Jesus' name. Their newfound faith caused them to suffer, but they embraced it, knowing persecution strengthened them in fellowship with their Lord and Savior.

This dynamic change can still happen today. It only takes a few families who will gather with a desire for the fullness of Christ to change a community, and indeed the world. Christian mutuality is a powerful dynamic and the impetus for explosive spiritual growth. But we are just as fallible as our predecessors who let their zeal slip away. The Apostle John warned the churches to encourage and admonish them so they would repent and make a fresh start with Gospel in its purity.

His warning applies to us today. It's human nature to slide into apathy. Let's take a look at the dedication of the first Christians to see how far we have fallen.

The newly baptized Christians devoted themselves to the apostles' teaching. They hung onto every word of Scripture and then applied it to their lives. They received the apostles' letters as if they were love letters, and they were eager to do what pleased their Bridegroom, Jesus Christ. The Lord's Table became a joyful celebration. They rejoiced in their remembrance of Christ and delightfully entered Jesus' presence to partake of His body and blood shed for the remission of sin. God's people were spiritually hungry. They consumed every word of instruction, confirmed what the apostles taught by searching the Scriptures, and they grew in grace and knowledge of their Lord and Savior.

The converts were feverish in their devotion to Christian fellowship. The community of believers shared everything they valued. They participated in joyful worship gatherings as if with one heart. With zealous faith they contributed from their own material goods for the benefit of the whole family of believers. They carried each other's burdens and prayed in earnest for one another. Where one was weak, they lent their strength. Every need was met because they filled what others lacked from their own resources. Everything they owned was dedicated to the cause of Christ.

The evening meal at the end of a long workday gave them a perfect excuse to get together. These common suppers were great bonding moments and came to be known as "love feasts." The bread and cup of the Lord's Table were part of their celebrative community dinners, and this served to bind them together in a stronger yoke of fellowship. If a family came to supper with no food to share—no problem. Generous people filled their empty plates.

The church began on a day they were gathered for prayer, and God's people continued this practice in earnest. They were eager to pray as a community and then watch Jesus' living and active presence at work among them. This kind of fervent and effective covenantal prayer is in agreement with God's will and word and is just as effective today. Prayers in community open the gates of heaven to accomplish all that God has purposed and planned. Praying together in one spirit is awesome, powerful, and encourages us in our private and personal prayers.

The early Christians were commended for their sincere hearts toward each other. Their open affections toward one another came about because of a great uniting influence—they gathered as one in Jesus' name. For them to cherish others in this way, they had to overcome their fallible human natures—traits opposed to esteeming others. We face the same challenge today. Personal differences caused disputes among them. But they chose to put aside their differences and imitate Christ. They refused to highlight the failures and weaknesses of other members and instead covered them in Christ's love.[1] In their gatherings they received pardon for sin and mercy, which inspired them to forgive and show compassion toward others. We should do no less than this in our gatherings today.

Christians in Jerusalem enjoyed the favor of all the people. Their neighbors, customers, masters, and governors saw Christ in them and the result-

---
1. 1 Peter 4:8.

ing miraculous change in their lives. The teaching of the word, community prayer, and the ministries of mercy and forgiveness in their gatherings spread out from there to affect everyone around them. They were a bright light, reflecting Christ in a dark world. They were the salt of the earth, and their saltiness benefited everyone with whom they rubbed elbows.

The first believers' hearts must have been supersized because they constantly welcomed people who were new to the faith. They opened their arms to over three thousand baptized believers in one day—and then more converts day after day. They did more than a quick greeting and pointing the new converts to a chair. They opened the doors of their hearts, the doors of their homes, welcomed them to their dinner tables, and drew them into the fellowship of God's precious Son. The new-born Christians were eager to grow in the spirit and wanted to be taught the disciplines of a Christian life. They were zealous to grow in grace and knowledge, and they spread the Good News with great enthusiasm.

The first Christians showed us the true heart of Christ. Even today, when people of Christian faith come together, and the Good News is preached in accord with all righteousness, the effect is a dramatic change in hearts and lives. The Gospel message is light and life to all who will hear, receive, and obey the call to believe and be baptized.[2] New converts are baptized into Christ and His body and made part of the fellowship of the church. Signs and wonders are given by means of spiritual gifts to confirm that the true promise of the Gospel is taught and received.

> *How shall we escape if we ignore so great a salvation? This salvation, which was first announced by the Lord, was confirmed to us by those who heard him. God also testified to it by signs, wonders and various miracles, and by gifts of the Holy Spirit distributed according to his will.*
> (Hebrews 2:3–4)

Now consider the manifest power of the Gospel that serves as a great equalizer in our fellowship gatherings. Poor beggars, wealthy merchants, laborers, farmers, or craftsmen—we are all called to come together to worship, minister, and serve as one people before a holy God. No one is exalted above another. A worship assembly serves to make us one in Christ. Some will come with plenty, a few will come in financial crisis, some may show up with a few nickels left in their pocket. Worshippers may come in spiritual poverty or with a mature knowledge of Christ. But we all come to worship in the presence of our High Priest, Jesus Christ, and receive His ministries according to our need.

---

2. Mark 16:16.

We are like many different cups poured into one vessel, who is Christ. Our Lord Jesus then pours His holy presence into us. We come into community to bless and receive His blessings. Every worshipper is gifted as the Spirit wills to attend or receive according to their provision or need. The power of gathering together becomes very real when it flows out as each one departs. We become like salt and light for our towns, states, nation, and the world.

The apostles' teaching shows us there is no need to exalt one over another. There will be no exploitation of the weak; instead, the weak are strengthened. Only Christ is exalted. Self-centered ambitions are left behind in favor of a Christ-like order that fosters sweet fellowship.

The Apostle Paul sought to establish order out of chaos by convincing the people in his day of their sin and their need of Christ. They had slipped back to their old ways and became disconnected from Christ, the Head of the church. This divide devastated their fellowship. Christ, the Head, is the impulse, authority, and the life blood of the church, and we must remain in Christ for fellowship to flourish. The Spirit of Christ is the teacher, comforter, vitality, and conscience of the church. But the distractions of the world make it too easy to abandon worship gatherings. Fellowship in Christ requires too much self-sacrifice. We tend to let the vertical spiritual connection slip away, and then the horizontal connections begin to crumble also. Paul encouraged them to come back to true fellowship so that God would be exalted.

> *Accept one another, then, just as Christ accepted you,*
> *in order to bring praise to God.*
> (Romans 15:7)

Look at how the beauty of their gatherings turned to ashes over time. The people became complacent in their saving faith, and their individual and collective zeal slipped away. The Apostle Paul warned them in a letter:

> *I am astonished that you are so quickly deserting the one who called you to live in the grace of Christ and are turning to a different gospel–*
> *which is really no gospel at all.*
> (Galatians 1:6–7)

The people began to depend on their own resources to accomplish the work of the church, and the fellowship suffered because of it. They slipped back into dependence on Hebraic Law for righteousness. Paul issued a stern accusation because of their serious regressive behavior. He needed to jar them awake with harsh words: "You foolish Galatians!"[3] Christ's followers fell into neglect of their worship gatherings, and they needed to be warned against apathy.

---
3. Galatians 3:1.

> *Not giving up meeting together, as some are in the habit of doing.*
> (Hebrews 10:25)

Their back peddling went full speed. At first, they welcomed the ministries of the gifts of the Spirit in signs and wonders that confirmed the truth of what the apostles taught. Then they regressed into resting on their laurels. Their regressive behavior prompted Paul to warn them not to despise prophecies or forbid some gifts of the Spirit. The Apostle John warned them not to forget their first love. The people became factious and formed cliques. Fellowship turned into arguments over the meaning of words. They dragged their opponents into public court to resolve their squabbles. Genealogies became more important than their position in Christ. Those who dropped out of fellowship became easily deceived because they were not grounded in the holy Scriptures.

Their backwards slide caused chaos, and selfish ambitions undermined the fellowship they enjoyed at first. Their self-serving ambitions showed that they loved the ways of the world more than the narrow path of God's kingdom. The Apostle John warned them, but he also encouraged them to overcome by the blood of the Lamb for the sake of Christian fellowship.

> *If we claim to have fellowship with him and yet walk in the darkness,*
> *we lie and do not live out the truth. But if we walk in the light,*
> *as he is in the light, we have fellowship with one another,*
> *and the blood of Jesus, his Son, purifies us from all sin.*
> (1 John 1:6–7)

The Apostle John's warning and encouragement also fits us today. We are called to leave behind deceit and darkness to walk in truth and light. This is an urgent call! Today is the day to return to our first love—Christ and the message of the cross. A refreshed passion for the Good News will once again strengthen our Christian fellowship. The joy of our gatherings is enriched when we fully embrace the ministries of our High Priest. There is no better hour than this to enter into the fullness of joyful fellowship in our Lord and Savior.

This is a plea to us to devote ourselves to the preaching of the Gospel of Jesus Christ for the good of fellowship. We must rekindle the joy of breaking bread together in the presence of Christ at the Lord's Table. Gathering for united prayer opens the gates so we may rise up in fellowship like a mighty army. How can we refuse to be infused with the Spirit's power for the battle ahead of us? As we enter into true fellowship, we will accomplish all God has purposed and planned for us. As we come into an orderly community we stand as equals before Christ, and our personal agendas are set aside for the good of all. Regular worship assemblies build trust in our Lord Jesus and in each other. Getting together offers us a taste of heaven and serves to adorn Christ's bride for His return. Gathering around a table for shared meals creates a bond that is a gift with eternal blessings.

Consider the apostles' warnings against self-promoting acts that destroy Christian fellowship. Turn from self-centered ambitions and serve the cause of Christ. We are taught to think of others above ourselves to receive the comfort ministered by the Spirit to our community of faith. To strengthen the communion of saints, we are called to assemble in fellowship as servants with the attitude of Christ. We are admonished to put aside our own agenda and enter into sweet fellowship to serve with one spirit and purpose. We must put aside our own ideas and come together so we may all benefit from the tender and compassionate ministries of our High Priest, Jesus Christ. To humble ourselves and assemble to pray with one heart and one mind is a powerful act that will soon make us witnesses of God's mighty right arm at work on behalf of His people. God's power is best manifested in humble servants who serve for the advancement of God's kingdom.

The church is built upon the Rock, Christ Jesus, and we must remain anchored in Him to enjoy fellowship in the Holy Spirit. Jesus ministers to us, His church, and strengthens our sweet communion by the power of selfless love. We are instructed to take on the nature of a servant to serve the community of faith for the glory of God the Father. This kind of dynamic fellowship sticks with us even as we depart from our gatherings. When we assemble in Jesus' name, we shine in His light like in the glow of the mid-day sun. As we go out from our gatherings, we mirror Christ like a supermoon that reflects the sun. The power of Christian fellowship is carried with us to change home life, communities, states, and nations.

Together we embrace our Lord Jesus in His passion for the cross and the saints who suffer to advance the Gospel. In Christ we enter into the fellowship of the cross. The Apostle Paul wrote to the church in Philippi to tell them of his desire for fellowship with Christ in His sufferings.[4] John the Baptizer showed us the heart and mind of a servant. This first-love kind of attitude serves to strengthen our fellowship in Christ.

He must become greater; I must become less.
(John 3:30)

---

4. Philippians 3:10–11.

When we humble ourselves and come together as one, with the heart and mind of our Savior, this serves to strengthen our fellowship in Christ and His body, the church.

15. Fellowship in Gathering
Q & A

1. Describe an attitude of heart that nurtures faith and fellowship.

2. What dangerous attitudes cause a gathering to slide into chaos?

3. Was the power of gathering together only for the early church?

4. What actions were evident in the first Christians that showed their love and zeal for Christ?

My Journal Notes:

Chapter 16
A Bond of Love

Key Scriptures:

- "A new command I give you: Love one another. As I have loved you, so you must love one another. By this everyone will know that you are my disciples, if you love one another." (John 13:34–35)

- "Be devoted to one another in love. Honor one another above yourselves." (Romans 12:10)

- "May the Lord make your love increase and overflow for each other and for everyone else, just as ours does for you." (1 Thessalonians 3:12)

- "We ought always to thank God for you, brothers and sisters, and rightly so, because your faith is growing more and more, and the love all of you have for one another is increasing." (2 Thessalonians 1:3)

- "And now these three remain: faith, hope and love. But the greatest of these is love." (1 Corinthians 13:13)

- "And over all these virtues put on love, which binds them all together in perfect unity." (Colossians 3:14)

Stories of David and his mighty men offer us beautiful examples of God's love that binds us together. When we read the historic accounts of David, we see glimpses of Christ. As a shepherd boy, he slayed lions and bears that threatened the flock. This prepared him to slay the giant Goliath with a slingshot and stone when he was a young man. After slaying the giant, he served King Saul, but finally had to flee from the king's jealous anger. After years of hiding out in the desert, he became king of all the tribes of Israel. His life provides lessons for our lives, so let's take a look at David in the Judean desert.

When David fled for his life to escape Saul's death threats, he hid in the wilderness of Ziph. It didn't take long for over four hundred men who were desperate, in debt, and in great distress, to find David and gather around him. Among these men, thirty-seven rose up to be renowned as David's "mighty men." They came as fugitives from enslavement for their debts. The tax man knocked on their doors back home. Crop failure forced them to sell the farm to pay their debts. Some of them had offended the king. The dropouts, failures, and the objects of town gossip came to join the horde. They fled to David, where they could leave their troubles behind. David rose up to lead them, and with him they were free from the troubles that dogged at their heels. David was a breath of fresh air. He was a fugitive just like them, and he understood each man's plight.

These misfits became a band of comrades. They all looked to David to find freedom from the king's reprisals. The bonds of love and affection grew because of the predicaments they held in common. The men camped out, ate, sang, celebrated, and laughed like a family. One man's burden was every man's burden. David's songs rang out from them as a chorus, echoing from the walls on the caves of their hideout. They brawled like brothers. The renegades fought to defend their comrades. A common homesickness united them as they chatted around the night fires. This next part of their story illustrates the extent of this bond of love.[1]

Three of David's mighty men heard him say how he thirsted for water from his hometown's well. He felt homesick for the pastures of his homeland. When they heard this, they must have looked at each other, girded on their swords, and snuck off to Bethlehem—now a stronghold of the Philistine army. No problem! The three men took swords in hand and fought off a whole army. Then they collected cool water from the well and took it back to David at their hideout. Because of their bond of love, they risked their lives so David could satisfy his thirst for the hometown's fresh, clear water.

Now, let's join David's troops as they gather around the night campfires. They collect in small groups with flames flickering on their ruddy faces. Listen up and hear their hearty laughter and a few slaps on the back as they tell stories of their exploits. The roasted wild goat meat gets passed around for each to cut off their share. Then, satisfied with bread and meat, they settle back and sing David's songs as the desert landscape darkens with the setting sun. Their voices may be out of tune, but their chant is beautiful because of the joy and love that reflects in their faces.

In a very real sense, this is a picture of what gathering in Jesus' name should look like, even if we're hiding out in a cave. We sing with one voice, pray in harmony, worship as a family, and share food and refreshment like kin. In our assemblies, one person's trouble is everyone's burden. When one of us is sick, we strengthen them with care, compassion, and fervent prayer. Those who mourn are comforted as we all grieve with them. As one in Christ, and according to God's word, we admonish our brothers and sisters with caring, tactful, and loving words.

A love like this is a sacrificial giving of ourselves for the good of the whole. We become recognized as disciples of Jesus because of our love for our brothers and sisters in Christ. Our devotion for each other is a hallmark of this bond of love. The honor we show for those who gather with us sets us apart

---
1. 2 Samuel 23.

from an ordinary get together. As newcomers enter our gatherings, they will sense Jesus' holy presence. Visitors will no longer say, "Where is their God?" Instead they will declare, "God is truly among them."

Jesus' manner of love binds us together in affection, while man-made varieties tend to tear us apart. Our Father's love leads us to true intimacy, while the artificial offers an empty affection.

Like seeds from meadow flowers, Christ's love spreads out in our worship gatherings. How can a bond of love be nurtured in isolation? Loving fellowship is fostered by forgiveness and mercy that we each minister to our brothers and sisters who come together in Jesus' name. Those who receive abundant pardons for sin tend to overflow with love for the One who forgives. Forgiveness and mercy are the nourishment that causes love to blossom into a bond of mutual affection. The Apostle Paul wrote to the Ephesian church to strengthen them, saying:

> *Be kind and compassionate to one another, forgiving each other,*
> *just as in Christ God forgave you.*
> (Ephesians 4:32)

The beauty of this bond of love is that it grows exponentially. The love of Christ in us will increase and overflow until each person is washed in it. Together we enter heaven's gates with thanksgiving, grateful to be brought into this covenant of love. With songs of praise, we enter into courts of the tabernacle of worship, delighted to be brought into the ministries of loving fellowship. In this community of faith, we encourage each other in hope, and love is what binds us all together in perfect unity—in Jesus' name.

The love David's men shared grew in a bond of common weakness, and they became mighty men who achieved impossible feats in the power of the Spirit. The victories they won were impossible, even with their combined human strength. David's three men didn't fight off the whole Philistine army because they got a huge adrenaline rush. They fought off the enemy soldiers motivated by a bond of godly love, and in the power in the Spirit. David's mighty men show us that there is no human measure of love, nor any mortal strength, that could overcome such impossible odds.

This kind of love is the greatest of all gifts to the church. God's love is superior to the offices of the church and more dynamic than all the spiritual gifts combined. It's a miraculous love that restores wounded souls, heals broken hearts. It is the fruit of the righteousness of Jesus Christ at work in our hearts and souls. God brought this to light on the first day of creation, and its power drives back the darkness of hate and bitterness. The Creator's love is a protective, caring, and watchful kind of love.

This is the power of love. You too may enter into this bond of affection in worshipful gatherings in Jesus' name.

16. A Bond of Love
Q & A

1. Why is it that abundant forgiveness inspires strong bonds of love?
   _____
   _____
   _____

2. How is it that a bond of weakness can lead us to a shared devotion that conquers all?
   _____
   _____
   _____

3. Why is godly love greater than faith and hope?
   _____
   _____
   _____

My Journal Notes:

Chapter 17
Gathering in Shalom [1]

Key Scriptures:

- "Let the peace of Christ rule in your hearts, since as members of one body you were called to peace. And be thankful." (Colossians 3:15)

- "If it is possible, as far as it depends on you, live at peace with everyone." (Romans 12:18)

- "Hold them in the highest regard in love because of their work. Live in peace with each other." (1 Thessalonians 5:13)

There is no more meaningful or beautiful greeting than "Shalom." Whether said as "hello" or "farewell," this salutation offers blessings of peace, harmony, wholeness, unity, prosperity, well-being, and tranquility. In western cultures, Christmas is a special season of the year to proclaim, "Peace on earth, and good will towards men." Some people offer a holy "kiss of peace" as they greet one another every day.

The search for peace is rampant. Service clubs send out calls for international peace conferences. Advocacy groups like Greenpeace promote their agendas for this planet to be sustained in peace. We sing out with songs of peace: "Let there be peace on earth, and let it begin with me."[2] Every family wants to raise their children in a peaceful world. We pray for our leaders so "that we may live peaceful and quiet lives."[3] And yet, peace eludes us because we search for it in all the wrong places.

The consequence of our misplaced quest is an epidemic of domestic violence. Gangs stain our streets with blood. Our system of justice doesn't offer impartiality to the poor. Corruption is rampant in state and national bureaucracies. The United Nations looks on, helpless, and issues warnings of an "increasingly chaotic" world. Wars rage on almost every continent. Trade wars, currency wars, border disputes, centuries old tribal conflicts, religious tyranny, and hostile corporate takeovers all add to the world's unruly nature. Fruitful land is exploited and turned into desert wasteland.[4] All of these hostilities add to the exponential growth of turmoil.

Even Jesus, the Prince of Peace said:

---
1. Shalom means peace in Hebrew.
2. Jill Jackson and Sy Miller, composers, "Let There Be Peace On Earth," 1971.
3. 1 Timothy 2:2.
4. Jeremiah 4:26, Micah 7:13.

> *"Do not suppose that I have come to bring peace to the earth.*
> *I did not come to bring peace, but a sword."*
> (Matthew 10:34)

Jesus' statement is the heart of this study.

Now we'll apply this principle to our assemblies where we come into His holy presence. Indeed, our Lord brandishes His sword of justice to separate us from the fellowship of darkness,[5] and He brings us into the fellowship of the Light of Christ,[6] the Prince of Peace.

One of the most wondrous moments in all of time occurred as shepherd priests on the night watch guarded flocks of the sacrificial lambs.

> *Suddenly a great company of the heavenly host appeared with the angel, praising God*
> *and saying, "Glory to God in the highest heaven,*
> *and on earth peace to those on whom his favor rests."*
> (Luke 2:13–14)

This is the glorious moment the prophets of old proclaimed and looked forward to seeing. Hundreds of years before the angel appeared to the shepherds, God sent His prophets to proclaim the coming Messiah to His people. Every word of prophecy was fulfilled, and the promise of peace came as a child. The Light of peace entered earth's realm in human form, born in a stable, and placed in a manger. But this is just the beginning of this miraculous story. Through Christ, we are reconciled to our heavenly Father by means of a blood-bought peace.

> *For God was pleased to have all his fullness dwell in him, and through him to reconcile to himself all things, whether things on earth or things in heaven, by making peace through his blood, shed on the cross.*
> (Colossians 1:19–20)

Today, peace for the Sabbath is proclaimed in the greeting: "Shabbat shalom." "Umevorach" is spoken in return to bid peace and blessings for the day. To say "Shalom Aleichem" is to speak peace. But the most common, everyday greeting is a clear and simple, "Shalom." This word encompasses us with peace and blessings of harmony. As we greet each other with the peace of Christ, we declare that we are one in Christ, we are reconciled to Him, and we share a holy love that is a precious gift from above. All God's children of faith find peace in forgiveness and cleansing. Because of this, as we speak shalom to our brothers and sisters, we proclaim the forgiveness of sins and the peace we have come to know.

---
5. 2 Corinthians 6:14.
6. 1 John 1:7.

True blessings are spoken from the heart. But when our hearts are disturbed, it's not easy to speak these precious words. By the time five o'clock rolls around on Friday many of us feel like we've been up to our necks in alligators, and our attempt to drain the swamp only made them mad. The company merger is a mess, quotas haven't been met, a key machine in the production line broke down, code for the new computer system has a major glitch, the subcontractor didn't show up, the shipment didn't arrive on time, and now the boss demands overtime. After a week in the swamp, how is it possible to have peace and greet others with peace?

It's a good thing for us that the Creator of the Universe invented weekend rest. After forty or more hours of hard work, our strength is exhausted, and we need a break. Peace and quiet is necessary to settle down and clear our minds. Cheering our kids as they play soccer or putting our feet up to cheer for our favorite football team are both great distractions, but they still don't offer the lasting peace we long for. A weekend trip to visit family can be a nice diversion, but not always peaceful.

Weekends are great, but they're only a tiny sample of real and eternal peace. How can we enter this forever rest? Who is the source of peace that sticks with us as we go back into the corporate jungle on Monday morning? How is it possible to find peace, let alone spread God's peace to others? Our Lord Jesus provides the answers to all these questions as He takes His sword in hand. The work of His double-edged blade is to judge with justice. The word of His mouth is His sword. This is the weapon used to separate us from the dark turmoil of this world that would destroy us.

For the word of God is alive and active. Sharper than any double-edged sword, it penetrates even to dividing soul and spirit, joints and marrow; it judges the thoughts and attitudes of the heart.
(Hebrews 4:12)

After Adam and Eve sinned, the Lord drove them from the garden and posted an angel with sword in hand to guard the way to the tree of life. The angelic guard did not block the way but guarded the way. He protects the way to Christ our Savior who is the Tree of Life. This guardian cherub safeguarded the way so the first couple, and all who followed them, could come to Jesus by faith alone and enter into God's eternal rest.

After he drove the man out, he placed on the east side of the Garden of Eden cherubim and a flaming sword flashing back and forth to guard the way to the tree of life.
(Genesis 3:24)

By faith we partake of the Tree of Life, and we are adopted into the family of God. As sons and daughters of the Most High God, we are called to gather in the presence of the Prince of Peace. Where just a few are gathered in Jesus' name we are lifted up into His holy presence. We gather together in Christ to be reconciled to those who share our faith. We are blessed as we minister peace, and speak peace, to those whose hearts are in turmoil.

> *"Blessed are the peacemakers, for they will be called children of God."*
> (Matthew 5:9)

Our Lord and Savior takes up His double-edged sword, which is His word, and powerfully separates us from chaos of darkness to bring us into the glorious light of peace.[7] His sword is prepared to defend us against the terrors that steal away the night's peace.[8] We must be separated to Christ and leave all else behind as we come to receive the blessings of shalom, and proclaim the gift of shalom. This salutation is part of how we prepare our hearts to come to the Lord's Table in peace and harmony to partake of Christ. We find peace together when we gather as one in Jesus' holy name.

At the beginning of His ministry, Jesus warned about the sword He brandished. But later, with the work of the cross finished, with blood-bought peace secured, and before ascending to the right hand of the Father, he said:

> *"Peace I leave with you; my peace I give you. I do not give to you as the world gives. Do not let your hearts be troubled and do not be afraid."*
> (John 14:27)

Jesus spoke shalom to His followers. He held out to them, and to us, a gift of peace. But two thousand years after Jesus ascended to the Father, the world still cannot provide peace to its inhabitants. Jesus teaches us to not to let our hearts be distressed or fearful, even in the middle of a storm. In trials and turmoil, His sword of justice is a comfort. Jesus also warned us that in this world we will have trouble.[9] Because of what He taught, we know that this temporal realm is the wrong place to search for peace. We must rise above the dust and turmoil of this world to enter into His realm of peace—the kingdom of the Son. It's as if we live in the eye of a storm. Violent winds whip around us, but we are hidden in the hollow of His hands where there is great peace. Though the earth shakes, our feet are safely set upon the Rock.

The work of Jesus' sword serves to sever us from the world's hostilities, strife, discord conflict, and from all that would bring us harm. He is mighty in

---

7. 1 Peter 2:9.
8. Song of Songs 3:8.
9. John 16:33.

battle and carries us as victors into His peace. The sword of His mouth breaks the chains of sin and cuts the cords of darkness that bind us. Jesus' sword serves to reconcile us to himself.

Coming out of his mouth is a sharp sword with which to strike down the nations. He will rule them with an iron scepter. He treads the winepress of the fury of the wrath of God Almighty.
(Revelation 19:15)

As we gather together in Jesus' name, we are lifted up into the holy presence of the Prince of Peace.

Shalom

---

17. Gathering in Shalom
Q & A

1. What are the consequences of looking for peace in all the wrong places?

2. Why did Jesus say: "I did not come to bring peace, but a sword"?

3. What is the most meaningful aspect of Shalom for you personally?

My Journal Notes:

Chapter 18
A Harmonious Chorus

Key Scriptures:

- "I will declare your name to my brothers and sisters; in the assembly I will sing your praises." (Hebrews 2:12)
- "Let the message of Christ dwell among you richly as you teach and admonish one another with all wisdom through psalms, hymns, and songs from the Spirit, singing to God with gratitude in your hearts." (Colossians 3:16)

Singing in a chorale is a great delight. The bass singers add a pleasing undertone to carry the song. A mezzo soprano's voice rings out with clear, glass-shattering notes. The soprano's melody and the alto's harmony anchor the song, and the tenors pitch in with notes that bring the music together. But they don't vocalize any old notes. There is a harmony maker who stands in front of them as a conductor or director. The random notes of an orchestra sound chaotic as each musician tunes their instrument before a concert. Then, with a tap and swing of a baton, the conductor brings them all together in harmony to create delightful, playful, exhilarating, and even mournful music.

These common examples lead us to a greater reality—worshipful spiritual songs sung in harmony with the Spirit of Jesus as conductor. When we sing in unison with the Spirit of Christ, our hearts and souls are joined together in the joy of the Lord. These harmonious songs are worth carrying with us to echo in our hearts and minds as we work, play, and enter the battlefront.

It is excellent in every way for us to sing before the Lord in the morning, mid-day, and evening.

> *From the rising of the sun to the place where it sets,*
> *the name of the Lord is to be praised.*
> (Psalm 113:3)

When we hum any old melody it's good for heart and soul. Our well-being benefits from crooning a tune. But we can go beyond common value of singing popular songs to find uncommon blessings of eternal value. The beauty of worshipful singing to the Lord in the shower, or on a hike in a field, forest or mountain top is awe-inspiring. But when we gather together in worshipful song, it's an even greater spiritual blessing. The gift of God's people singing out as one with worship and praise, each in his or her own unique voice, is too wonderful to neglect. Indeed, we become spiritually impoverished when we disregard gathering together to offer worshipful praises before the Lord Almighty.

In a worship gathering, we sing and lift up holy hands to the Lord, and this is a delightful and uplifting part of exalting Christ. Even more than this, when we gather together in Jesus' name, the Holy Spirit encompasses us as a congregation and inspires us with words of praise.

> *Be filled with the Spirit, speaking to one another with psalms, hymns, and songs from the Spirit. Sing and make music from your heart to the Lord, always giving thanks to God the Father for everything, in the name of our Lord Jesus Christ.*
> (Ephesians 5:18–20)

When we come together to worship with voices and instruments, this is a time that serves to unite our hearts in song. While the congregation voices the beautiful words of the Psalms and the words of inspired song writers, our souls are gladdened and our spirits uplifted. Tithes and sacrificial offerings presented with glad hearts in our assembly inspire us in joyful song. A gathering around the Lord's Table to receive His body that was broken, and partake of the cup of His blood that was shed for the forgiveness of our sins, is to take part in a miracle that arouses our hearts to sing His praises.

Celebrating together with a new brother or sister who follows the Lord Jesus in baptism makes us witnesses of one of the greatest miracles of the kingdom of heaven. The joy of our salvation ought to cause our souls to rejoice in joyful songs of celebration.

> *Praise the Lord, my soul; all my inmost being, praise his holy name.*
> (Psalm 103:1)

Greeting your brothers and sisters with a holy embrace and words of peace is a blessing that will wash over you like a sweet song. Gathering together to pray for each other, to share our needs, and bear each other's burdens, will lift up our brothers and sisters in Christ. Like clefs of music rising in the winds of the Spirit, we will lift up our voices in thanksgiving. Sharing in prayerful intercessions ought to put a hopeful dance in our step.

For those of us who are part of a gathering, elders are available to pray for forgiveness and healing.[1] Their healing touch is like sweet music to the suffering soul. The elder's prayer of faith is like a refreshing melody. It's a petition that inspires a song of thanksgiving in our hearts.

As we gather together to sing with gratitude in our hearts, we are re-

---

1. James 5:14–16.

freshed in the Holy Spirit. We become one in fellowship as we speak to each other with psalms, hymns, and spiritual songs that glorify His holy name.

Glorify the Lord with me; let us exalt his name together.
(Psalm 34:3)

Spontaneous and inspired songs, sung in the Spirit, will flow from our hearts to enrich soul and spirit of all who are gathered. Making worshipful music before the Lord together gives us a sweet taste of the throng of voices in heaven's choir that fill eternity with joyful song.

A great blessing is in store for us as we gather to lift up our voices with songs of worship. When we sing out the Gospel's message of grace, the words are written in our hearts. Our worshipful words and music combine to write the truths of Scripture indelibly in our memory, and then we can carry our songs of joy, exaltation, and rejoicing with us to strengthen us until we gather again. Indeed, the celebrative refrains we lift with our voices go before us.

The awesome impact of Scripture's truths brought together with our collective voices will last even after the last note is sung. When we are sent out from our gatherings it's often like we are sent into battle. King Jehoshaphat knew the power in songs of praise and worship, and he took the choir into battle.

After consulting the people, Jehoshaphat appointed men to sing to the Lord and to praise him for the splendor of his holiness as they went out at the head of the army, saying: "Give thanks to the Lord, for his love endures forever."
(2 Chronicles 20:21)

The battle and the battlefield are the Lord's, and our songs of praise go out before us into victory. God who is mighty in battle won a great victory that day, and the armies of the Lord returned home with songs of exaltation.

Then, led by Jehoshaphat, all the men of Judah and Jerusalem returned joyfully to Jerusalem, for the Lord had given them cause to rejoice over their enemies.
(2 Chronicles 20:27)

When the battles are all won, and the final victory is ours, we will enter into the joy of the Lord, and with all the saints we will sing in a choir with ten thousands of voices forever.

And they sang a new song before the throne and before the four living creatures and the elders.
(Revelation 14:3)

*After this I heard what sounded like the roar of a great multitude in heaven shouting:
"Hallelujah! Salvation and glory and power belong to our God,
for true and just are his judgments".*
(Revelation 19:1–2)

*Together we enter a time of singing, a time for expressing our love like the song of a
bride who gathers springtime blossoms for the One she loves.
Flowers appear on the earth; the season of singing has come.*
(Song of Songs 2:12)

In Jesus' name, we gather where praise and worship will bring us together in harmonious melody. When a congregation gathers in Jesus' name, our Lord Jesus joins with us, and together we sing His new song of love and joyful fellowship. Let us join hands with our Lord Jesus and sing out in jubilant harmony. Even singing as we wake in the morning.

Let his faithful people rejoice in this honor and sing for joy on their beds.
(Psalm 149:5)

And then, from the moment our feet hit the floor to the moment we close our eyes at night, let the songs of praise and worship sung in the assembly flow from our hearts and well up from our mouths.

Of course, enjoy the fun and common melodies you like. It's good for your health to croon, even if it's country music. But more than this, sing out songs of praise and worship, and your soul and spirit will be strengthened. The effect lasts forever. The songs you sing in a gathering will stick with you and lift your spirit like a rhapsody of joy. Sing in the shower, sing while you're driving, and no one will care if you sing out of tune. Burst out with thanksgiving in your heart while making pancakes for the kids. Vocalize your heart filled with praise even while you take out the garbage. Chortle out a sweet song of Jesus to your baby while you bathe him. In fellowship with Christ Jesus you are blessed with so many good reasons to burst out with song.

Christian gatherings offer scores of occasions to lift up songs of praise and worship with voices and instruments. Our hearts have cause to sing when we witness the bounty of the Lord's Table. Gifts and offerings presented to the Lord with glad hearts offer us a great reason to burst out in song. When we witness the miracle of God's saving grace, it will lift our spirits to shout out with verses of exaltation to the Lord our Savior.

Then my soul will rejoice in the Lord and delight in his salvation.
(Psalm 35:9)

The words of the holy Scriptures ministered in a gathering will inspire our soul and spirit to overflow with words of praise. The truths we sing will go before us as we are sent out to do battle—and the victory is the Lord's.

Praise the Lord.

Praise God in his sanctuary; praise him in his mighty heavens.
Praise him for his acts of power; praise him for his surpassing greatness.
Praise him with the sounding of the trumpet, praise him with the harp and lyre,
praise him with timbrel and dancing, praise him with the strings and pipe,
praise him with the clash of cymbals, praise him with resounding cymbals.

Let everything that has breath praise the Lord.

Praise the Lord.

(Psalm 150)

---

18. A Harmonious Chorus
Q & A

1. What is the beneficial effect of singing together with the Spirit of Christ?

2. How is it that gathering together in Jesus' name inspires us to worship with psalms, hymns, and spiritual songs?

3. Describe the lasting power of song after the last note is sung in a worship assembly.

My Journal Notes:

Chapter 19
The Power of Prayer Gatherings

Key Scriptures:

- "Again, truly I tell you that if two of you on earth agree about anything they ask for, it will be done for them by my Father in heaven." (Matthew 18:19)

- "Ask and it will be given to you; seek and you will find; knock and the door will be opened to you." (Matthew 7:7)

- "Rejoice always, pray continually, give thanks in all circumstances; for this is God's will for you in Christ Jesus." (1 Thessalonians 5:16–18)

Prayer, like flowing spring water, is a continuous part of life for God's people. Whether on our morning walk, on our commute to work, on Instagram enjoying family pictures, at the dinner table with family, or digging in the garden, everything we do is an occasion for prayer. And yet, the most powerful and effective intercessions are prayers in a gathering. Prayer assemblies with a common purpose, and in agreement with the word and the Spirit, are awesome and effective.

Our community prayer is more than a get-together to pray about a need, it is a triple threat against the kingdom of darkness. The will of the Spirit, the words of Scripture, and the desires God places in our hearts come together like a powerful flood. In our prayer assemblies, when we pray together in agreement, it's as if we walk with the Spirit of Jesus leading the way. Prayers in covenant serve to shepherd us into God's counsel, and we will pray with eternal effect. These effectual and fervent prayers are a sweet-smelling fragrance, collected like incense in golden bowls in the heavens.[1]

The church began in a prayerful gathering, and God's people who gather will continue to be strengthened for the work of the Great Commission in prayerful assemblies. The purpose of this chapter's study is to unify us as we gather in prayerful assemblies.

You've heard of a "meeting of the minds" when people come together to chart a course. Good things start to happen when everyone is in agreement and the boss gets on board with the project. A company that comes together to include janitors, shipping clerks, salespeople, line managers, account executives, COOs, CFOs, and CEOs, will achieve amazing success.

Christians are called to a greater kind of agreement, not of minds and

---
1. Revelation 5:8.

human energies alone, but souls and spirit brought together in the Spirit. The prophet Amos asked a pointed question as he called the people to come together:

> *Can two people walk together without agreeing on the direction?*
> (Amos 3:3 NLT)

When two or more people head the same direction in unified prayer, and in step with the desire God has put in their hearts, incredible strength is stirred up. The prophet Joel called a sacred assembly of the people. He brought the people together in repentance. When God's word, God's will, and God's desire come together with our will and desire, it's like connecting to the source of immense power. The prophet Elijah prayed in agreement with the Lord of Hosts with awesome effect.

> *Elijah was a human being, even as we are. He prayed in earnest that it would not rain, and it did not rain on the land for three and a half years.*
> (James 5:17)

Unified prayers and petitions lifted up to the heavens usher us into the realm of the miraculous. Lives are changed for all eternity. Suffering is ended and turned around so we can minister to the distressed. Broken people are made whole to become functioning parts within the body of Christ. Those who are torn are brought together and healed. What was dying springs to life. Hatred is turned around so mercy and loving kindness will win the day. The violent are exposed and brought to judgment. Grief is washed away, and the joy of the Lord takes its place. Anxiety turns to comfort and hope. Panic turns to a restful calm. Wounds are healed and hearts are restored. Lost and wandering souls are brought back to the Good Shepherd's fold. All these good things are brought about because of the power of our petitions prayed in agreement.

Consider the beauty of intercessions made in covenant with our Lord Jesus. The world around us is impacted as we pray the Scriptures in accord with God's purpose and plan. We can pray with confidence in accord with Isaiah's prophecy.

> *The Spirit of the Sovereign Lord is on me, because the Lord has anointed me to proclaim good news to the poor. He has sent me to bind up the brokenhearted, to proclaim freedom for the captives and release from darkness for the prisoners, to proclaim the year of the Lord's favor and the day of vengeance of our God, to comfort all who mourn, and provide for those who grieve in Zion–to bestow on them a crown of beauty instead of ashes, the oil of joy instead of mourning, and a garment of praise instead of a spirit*

of despair. They will be called oaks of righteousness, a planting of the Lord for the display of his splendor.
(Isaiah 61:1–3)

Jesus spoke these words as He proclaimed the prophecy fulfilled right before the people's eyes. Jesus hasn't changed and these words are still fulfilled in our day. These are powerful words to pray.

Think about it. As we meditate on this truth, we will see that God's power is manifested when we press our plea before the gates of heaven on behalf of the wounded and brokenhearted. It is also God's desire for wounds to be dressed and anointed with the healing oil of the Spirit. When we pray for those who mourn to receive the oil of joy, this is an awesome prayer of agreement with the word and Spirit. Prayers lifted up in harmony with the Word, our Savior and Redeemer, are a sweet-smelling fragrance before the throne of God. When our petitions come into unity with God's word, with the desire of the Spirit in unified prayer, we will be like a mighty army rising up from our prayer-bent knees to do battle in God's kingdom. The darkness will flee in the light of Christ. When we come together to pray in covenant, in accord with Jesus' name, we pray the effective and fervent prayers of righteous saints.

The prayer of a righteous person is powerful and effective.
(James 5:16)

As we come into agreement with all that is in Jesus' name, in accord with the righteousness of Jesus Christ, and when we pray together with God's purpose and plan, our prayers are effective to move the hand of God because we agree to walk in the same direction. This also means that the lives we live ought to be in agreement with the prayers we pray. Covenant prayers exemplify the whole gathering, and our collective actions ought to agree with what we pray.

Does our God and Father need our prayers before He acts on our behalf? Not at all! He is Sovereign over all. Because He has the nature of Abba Father,[2] a loving nature, and a desire to usher us into the counsel of His Spirit, He leads us into a bond of covenant as heirs of His kingdom and acts on our behalf through prayers of the saints.

One of the greatest examples of the effect of prayer is on the day of Pentecost when the church was established. All Jesus' disciples were gathered together in prayer.

---

2. Galatians 4:7.

> *When Pentecost came, they were all together in one place.*
> (Acts 2:1)

Jesus had already taught them how to pray. He taught them this discipline in order to reveal the Father's loving nature toward them.

> *"Blessed are the pure in heart, for they will see God."*
> (Matthew 5:8)

For over three years He instructed them, showed them the Father's heart, and sent them out in His power and authority to minister. Now, on this day, God's promise of a Comforter came together with the disciples who gathered together to pray. They lifted their petition to the heavens in agreement and in accord with all they were taught by Jesus, who is the Word of God. They emptied themselves before God in prayer as the Father prepared them to be filled with the Holy Spirit and with power. To this day, Pentecost stands as the greatest and most powerful prayer gathering of the church. They came together in agreement and prayed in accord with the heart, purpose, and promises of the Lord Almighty. The foundation of the church was set in place through the powerful effect of coming together in prayer. And on that day over three thousand men and their families heard the Gospel message, believed, and were baptized. This is the power and effect of prayer in covenant with Christ.

Before time began, Creator God knew every prayer that would be prayed, and every petition that would be lifted to the heavens. As God created the heavens and earth, He set the foundations of the earth, and the groundwork for all things upon the earth. To know the God of Creation, His nature, His purpose and plan, and then intercede in agreement and in accord with this plan is a timeless and powerful prayer. Creator God treasures the prayers of the saints and stores them up like incense.

> *And when he had taken the scroll, the four living creatures and the twenty-four elders fell down before the Lamb, each holding a harp, and golden bowls full of incense, which are the prayers of the saints.*
> (Revelation 5:8 ESV)

When we are too weak to lift our hands in prayer, we are strengthened together as we pray. We see an example of this when Aaron and Hur strengthened Moses while Joshua fought in battle.

When Moses' hands grew tired, they took a stone and put it under him and he sat on it. Aaron and Hur held his hands up—one on one side, one on the other—so that his hands remained steady till sunset.
(Exodus 17:12)

When Moses raised his hands with the staff of God, Joshua prevailed. But when Moses got tired and lowered his hands, the Amalekites started to prevail against Israel. By Moses' example we can see that God never intended for us to always stand alone in prayer.

When we pray in a gathering no one voice should always be preeminent. All who are present ought to add their voice as they agree with the prayer as it is lifted up. There is no need to only listen while another person prays. We can join our voices with them, not to eclipse their prayer but to strengthen their petitions. Orderly responses of "amen," "yes, Lord," "may it be, Lord," "hear our prayer," or other prayerful words of agreement will encourage the petitioner as they pray. The greatest prayer to unify all people of Christian faith is the prayer Jesus taught us to pray. We pray this prayer with great boldness and confidence, together with one voice. And our Lord Jesus joins together with us as we pray:

*"Our Father in heaven,
hallowed be your name, your kingdom come,
your will be done, on earth as it is in heaven.
Give us today our daily bread. And forgive us our debts,
as we also have forgiven our debtors. And lead us not into temptation,
but deliver us from the evil one."*
(Matthew 6:9–13)

In his letter to the Thessalonian church, the Apostle Paul instructed them to pray continually.[3] This letter shows us that the prayers we pray in a gathering go with us as we renew the prayers and persist in prayer. We can do this even while working to provide for our family. We can cast our cares upon the Lord[4] while we commute to work. We can call upon the Lord while the boss drones on at the board meeting. We can lift up prayerful appeals before the kids arrive for the class we're about to teach. A brisk morning walk provides a perfect time to sing out our petitions accompanied by the birds in the trees. God hears and answers our individual prayers and our private prayers wherever we are. Private prayer times are special because we can pray about things that only you and the Lord need to know about.

Our private prayers are encouraged and strengthened when we incor-

---
3. 1 Thessalonians 5:17.
4. 1 Peter 5:7.

porate community prayers. Confidence to pray effective personal prayers is bolstered as we carry the harmony of community prayer that occurred in our gatherings. Indeed, we are encouraged to pray with boldness when we witness God's answers to the prayers we prayed together in our worship assemblies.

When we come together to pray in agreement, we fill the holy sanctuary with fragrance and add sweet-smelling incense to heaven's golden bowls. Heart to heart, shoulder to shoulder, we will all advance like a mighty army in prayerful agreement. God's word and the Holy Spirit direct and inform our prayers. Together we stand in God's council to pray in accord with the heart of God, and this is a power packed and effective prayer.

Whether we pray together to agree on a need for repentance, or intercede in agreement with God's purpose, plans, and promises, when we come together and petition the Father in Jesus' holy name, the hand of God is moved. Indeed, He longs to show His arm strong on our behalf.[5]

Yet the Lord longs to be gracious to you; therefore he will rise up to show you compassion. For the Lord is a God of justice. Blessed are all who wait for him!
(Isaiah 30:18)

The disciples' prayers of agreement changed the world as the church was founded. Through our prayers of agreement, the church will also be strengthened to complete the work that began on that day—the work of the Great Commission. Be encouraged to pray the most powerful of prayers, lifted up as one voice in the congregation, the prayer the Lord taught us to pray. In our private time and throughout the day, we will find strength and encouragement as we recall the prayers from our gatherings.

Prayers, petitions, and intercessions are an awesome gift for God's people to reach out to the heavens. Our prayers are heaven's treasure, collected as a fragrant incense in heaven's golden bowls. When the trumpet sounds to call grandmas, grandpas, dads, moms, newlyweds, toddlers, infants, and our leaders to come together and pray, we must answer the call so we may be cleansed and strengthened in accord with God's grace, mercy, and forgiveness. The power of our united prayers will strengthen all of us to rise up from prayer-bent knees like a mighty army, victorious on the day of battle.

---

5. 2 Chronicles 16:9.

19. The Power of Prayer Gatherings
Q & A

1. Why are prayers offered in community a triple threat against the kingdom of darkness?

2. Describe the kind of agreement that is so vital as Christians come together to pray.

3. Why is it so important to pray in accord with God's word, His purpose, and in covenantal agreement with each other?

4. Why does God desire that we lift up our petitions to Him?

My Journal Notes:

Chapter 20
Together We Make Up What Is Lacking in Christ's Afflictions

Key Scriptures:

- "Now I rejoice in what I am suffering for you, and I fill up in my flesh what is still lacking in regard to Christ's afflictions, for the sake of his body, which is the church." (Colossians 1:24)

- "So do not be ashamed of the testimony about our Lord or of me his prisoner. Rather, join with me in suffering for the gospel, by the power of God." (2 Timothy 1:8)

- "Therefore I endure everything for the sake of the elect, that they too may obtain the salvation that is in Christ Jesus, with eternal glory." (2 Timothy 2:10)

- Additional study Scriptures: Romans 5:3–5; Hebrews 2:8–10; James 1:2, 1:12

Why do we suffer persecution as Christians? The suffering of Jesus the Christ is sufficient to cover the penalty of sin. So why must we endure the world's torments? Wasn't Jesus' passion for the cross sufficient affliction for all time?

When we realize that the work of the Great Commission is not finished, the answer becomes clear. The job given to us is far from accomplished. As Jesus' followers, we are called to do this good work, and we are brought together with Christ in His torments to press on toward the goal. As we persevere for the Gospel, we are made one with Him in His anguish, and all those who are one with Christ will be hated because of Christ in us.

Jesus suffered on our behalf on a cruel Roman cross. He was accused of blasphemy and rejected by the religious leaders of His day. And yet, He was willing to die on a cross to pay the penalty for our sin. Why then must we suffer as Christians? Didn't Jesus suffer for all the sins of the world for all time? And yet to suffer for Christ is a reality in our time. More than just a reality, the persecution accelerates exponentially as time marches on. To answer these questions, take a look at the world we live in. Too many nations are in the grip of terror, anarchy, and subjected to poverty. There are unreached tribes whose only witnesses are the sun, moon and stars. Too many language groups are without Bibles they can read and understand.

Is the work of the church finished? Is the work of the Gospel and the

Great Commission completed? It's quite obvious that it is not. There is so much work left to be done.

Our Lord Jesus founded the church, initiated it by His shed blood on the cross and an outpouring of the Holy Spirit. He filled our gatherings with blood-bought saints, and now advances the Gospel by means of the blood of all those who are called by His name. The Good News must be preached for all who have ears to hear because it's a message for every creature under heaven. The message excludes no one, and all people of every tribe, nation, people, and language group must hear of Jesus' saving grace and mercy. Whether or not they will accept the gift of faith, they must have an opportunity to hear sweet words of salvation. Until the work of the Great Commission is complete, we must fight on and pay the price. Listen to Jesus' words as He commissioned us for this good work of the church.

Then Jesus came to them and said, "All authority in heaven and on earth has been given to me. Therefore go and make disciples of all nations, baptizing them in the name of the Father and of the Son and of the Holy Spirit, and teaching them to obey everything I have commanded you.

> *And surely I am with you always, to the very end of the age."*
> (Matthew 28:18–20)

To be sure, our afflictions are not sufficient to wash away guilt and sin. The shed blood of the saints does not cleanse us of our sin. Nor can we earn our way into heaven through affliction. The work of Christ Jesus on the cross is sufficient for our salvation. No more is required to be made right before a holy God. And yet, to join together with the Spirit of Christ to complete the Great Commission work of the church, we must come together with Christ in His afflictions and endure for the Gospel. God's ambassadors are called to suffer for the cause of Christ as we press on toward the goal. As the finish line comes into sight the persecution of the church has hit that proverbial exponential curve.

Jesus warned us this would happen. It's as if Jesus was telling us not to take it personal. It is Christ in us and His church that the world hates.

> *"If the world hates you, keep in mind that it hated me first. If you belonged to the world, it would love you as its own. As it is, you do not belong to the world, but I have chosen you out of the world. That is why the world hates you."*
> (John 15:18–19)

The hatred shown toward Christians is nothing to be embarrassed about, but a cause for celebration.

> *If you suffer as a Christian, do not be ashamed,*
> *but praise God that you bear that name.*
> (1 Peter 4:16)

We express joy in sufferings because they serve to complete the Spirit's good work in our lives. The fruit of suffering is to grow us up in Christ.

> *Not only that, but we rejoice in our sufferings, knowing that suffering produces endurance, and endurance produces character, and character produces hope, and hope does not put us to shame, because God's love has been poured into our hearts through the Holy Spirit who has been given to us.*
> (Romans 5:3–5 ESV)

What is lacking in Christ's afflictions is that the work of Christ's sorrows is not complete until every tribe, nation, people, and language group has heard the Good News Gospel of Jesus Christ. We offer up our bodies as living sacrifices for this great purpose.

> *Therefore, I urge you, brothers and sisters, in view of God's mercy,*
> *to offer your bodies as a living sacrifice, holy and pleasing to God–*
> *this is your true and proper worship.*
> (Romans 12:1)

Whether locked in a cell like Aleksandr Solzhenitsyn, torn away from family and sent to a concentration camp like Corrie ten Boom, arrested and sentenced to death by hanging like Dietrich Bonhoeffer, or chained to a Roman guard in prison like the Apostle Paul, we are not alone because we are one with Christ—the whole body of Christ. The Apostle to the Gentiles calls for us to be unshakeable and strengthened together as a family in Christ.

> *Therefore, my brothers and sisters, you whom I love and long for,*
> *my joy and crown, stand firm in the Lord in this way, dear friends!*
> (Philippians 4:1)

We don't suffer alone because we're all in the same boat, going the same direction. Jesus' followers suffer as Christ's body, the church. Together we press forward as a mighty army to make straight the way for the Light of Life to redeem all who will hear the call. We strengthen each other for the battle. One takes up the sword of the Spirit and the shield of faith, while another offers up fervent prayers for their strength. Another will be sent out with Gospel shoes on their feet, with support and encouragement from their home gathering, and it is beautiful to see.

And how can anyone preach unless they are sent? As it is written:

> *"How beautiful are the feet of those who bring good news!"*
> (Romans 10:15)

All of us together are called to offer ourselves as living sacrifices, ready on the day of battle, even if it's necessary to shed blood for the cause of Christ and the Good News Gospel. There will continue to be a great cost in blood and lives until Christ's appointed day.

> *They will fall by the sword and will be taken as prisoners to all the nations. Jerusalem will be trampled on by the Gentiles until the times of the Gentiles are fulfilled.*
> (Luke 21:24)

Our sacrifice serves to join us together with our Savior in His passion. Yet we press on to lift up Jesus Christ to a lost and dying world so the work of the church may be completed. Together we press on to fulfill Jesus' calling to:

> *"Go and make disciples of all nations, baptizing them in the name of the Father and of the Son and of the Holy Spirit."*
> (Matthew 28:19)

We have good reason to rejoice when we suffer for the cause of Christ. As we forge ahead toward the finish line and fulfill the high calling of the Good News Gospel, we follow in the Apostle Paul's footsteps.

> *I press on toward the goal to win the prize for which God has called me heavenward in Christ Jesus.*
> (Philippians 3:14)

When we are hard pressed, we rejoice because we are strengthened to persevere. Our Lord Jesus builds character in us as we endure. In the strength of character, we find great hope. The world sees Christ is us and hates us because of it. Yet our hearts are glad because we are one with Christ in His suffering. The cause is great, and we push forward to see the day when Christ is revealed in His fullness. The Apostle Peter was familiar with these afflictions and wrote to encourage us:

> *In all this you greatly rejoice, though now for a little while you may have had to suffer grief in all kinds of trials. These have come so that the proven genuineness of your faith–of greater worth than gold, which perishes even though refined by fire–may result in praise, glory and honor when Jesus Christ is revealed.*
> (1 Peter 1:6–7)

In the anguish of persecution, we are made one with Christ and His body, the church. Persecution doesn't earn our salvation, yet in affliction we are given an awesome gift. Our eyes are opened to look forward to Christ revealed in all His glory and majesty.

*But rejoice inasmuch as you participate in the sufferings of Christ,
so that you may be overjoyed when his glory is revealed.*
(1 Peter 4:13)

---

20. Together we Make Up for What is Lacking in Christ's Afflictions Q & A

1. What does it mean to fill up in our flesh what is still lacking in regard to Christ's afflictions?

2. What is a living sacrifice?

3. Is the work of the Great Commission completed?

4. How is it even possible that persecution is a gift for Jesus' followers?

My Journal Notes:

Chapter 21
Forgiveness in Gathering

Key Scriptures:

- "Bear with each other and forgive one another if any of you has a grievance against someone. Forgive as the Lord forgave you." (Colossians 3:13)

- "Therefore confess your sins to each other and pray for each other so that you may be healed. The prayer of a righteous person is powerful and effective." (James 5:16)

- "Be kind and compassionate to one another, forgiving each other, just as in Christ God forgave you." (Ephesians 4:32)

- In this study we'll focus on forgiveness in our worship gatherings. This is the way of peace and the means of Shalom for community worship. An emphasis on forgiveness in our assemblies does not detract from daily prayers asking for forgiveness.

- And forgive us our sins, as we have forgiven those who sin against us. (Matthew 6:12 NLT)

God's forgiveness is both for the individual and for the community gathered for worship, and it's vital as we live out the Gospel of peace.[1] This study will lead us to know the power of forgiveness in a community of faith.

A burden of guilt can hang around our necks like a bag of rocks. Sin is like heavy black stones that bend our shoulders and hinder every step we take. But we become so used to the weight of our sin that we trudge on with our back bent, pretending it's no problem.

Is there no one who will shout out the truth? We can be set free from this burden of guilt! Have we somehow missed hearing the Good News that there is freedom for those who are captive to sin? Why do we stumble along without hope? But with blind determination we press on, wounded, embittered, and held down by the weight of our sin. But our sin not only harms us as individuals, it stains the whole body of Christ.

We ought to shout out the Gospel message like a news flash. Freedom for those who are captive to sin ought to be proclaimed at every intersection. This is the greatest news ever, and for good reason. We are all born with Adam's sinful nature. Like Eve, we have a sin debt, and there is no cover-up for our depravity. It's as if we're caught in a trap and can't fight our way out. But

---
1. Ephesians 6:15.

there is hope because our Lord Jesus, by means of His suffering on the cross, proclaimed freedom for those oppressed by sin.

> *"The Spirit of the Lord is on me, because he has anointed me to proclaim good news to the poor. He has sent me to proclaim freedom for the prisoners and recovery of sight for the blind, to set the oppressed free, to proclaim the year of the Lord's favor."*
> (Luke 4:18–19)

When we come into agreement with the prophetic words that Jesus read and then declared fulfilled, the weight of sin will lift from our shoulders. This freedom came at a great price. Jesus paid our sin debt with His shed blood. Everyone born into this world is caught in the clutches of Adam's sin and in need of Christ, our Redeemer. We follow in Adam's footsteps and sin against God every day of our lives. Our sin is an affront to our Savior, Jesus. This sin is against the body of Christ (the church), and our sin offends and brings harm to everyone who is called by Jesus' name. Jesus bought our freedom from sin by giving His body to be broken and His blood to be shed—His very life as He was nailed to the cross. Indeed, He gave His life to redeem our lives from the ravages of sin, Satan, and death. Because of the sin debt that Jesus paid, we have this great promise:

> *If we confess our sins, he is faithful and just and will forgive us our sins and purify us from all unrighteousness.*
> (1 John 1:9)

Sin's shackles drop from our feet when we are forgiven. With our eyes opened, we can see and receive this freedom from the debt of sin. The bag of rocks that entangled us is lifted from around our necks, and we can leap for joy—freed from the oppression of sin. The black stone that hangs around our neck is replaced with a small, white stone of mercy.[2]

Isaiah prophesied the freedom Jesus gained on our behalf. Our High Priest still bestows it today through His servants. When we confess our sin against God and ask for forgiveness, Jesus mediates between us and God.[3] Because of the reconciling blood of Christ, our Father in heaven says, "I forgive you." Our Lord Jesus speaks out what the Father is speaking,[4] and says, "I forgive you." The servant leaders in our gatherings are given the authority to echo Jesus' words and say, "I forgive you."

Jesus didn't end His ministry of reconciliation among us after He ascended to the right hand of the Father. Our Prince and Savior[5] continues this

---

2. Revelation 2:17.
3. 1 Timothy 2:5–6.
4. John 12:49.
5. Acts 5:31.

ministry in our day and time, serving as High Priest as we gather to worship. Before His ascension to the Father, Jesus prepared His disciples by ordaining authority in the church. He held out the "Key of David" and invested His apostles, and those who are called after them, with authority to minister and serve.

Remember that Jesus spoke only what He heard the Father speaking and ministered to those to whom the Father ministered. He did nothing on His own.[6] In the same way, those who are given authority in our gatherings will speak out the forgiveness Jesus is speaking. Apart from Christ they have no authority to proclaim these holy words. The Father gave Jesus His words of forgiveness, and Jesus gives the same words to those who are called to minister words of reconciliation and healing to all those who gather with repentant and contrite hearts.

> *Therefore, my friends, I want you to know that through Jesus*
> *the forgiveness of sins is proclaimed to you.*
> (Acts 13:38)[7]

First, by the power of God's word and the work of the Holy Spirit, we are led to confess our sin. Then, those who serve in Jesus' name breathe out His words of forgiveness to God's people. It may help to understand forgiveness in this way. With repentant hearts, we cross a threshold called Forgiveness. As we enter through this door, we come into a courtyard of reconciliation.[8] In this place we come into the riches of God's grace.[9] We are brought back to sweet fellowship with our heavenly Father, and once again, we can come before the throne of grace with boldness to lay our petitions before God Almighty.[10] We will hear our name called to come stand in God's council.[11] Jesus will take us by the hand to come dwell in His dwelling.[12]

What is the source of this abundant forgiveness? It is our Father in heaven who forgives us for the sake of his holy name. Father God gave this authority to His Son, who serves as our High Priest. Then, those who serve under the authority of Christ, speak words of reconciliation in our local gatherings to repentant hearts.

The one who proclaims forgiveness breathes out the very words of Christ and speaks the words of the Father for sin to be pardoned. Those whom God

---

6. John 5:30.
7. Also see Acts 26:18.
8. 2 Corinthians 5:18–21.
9. Ephesians 1:7.
10. Hebrews 4:16.
11. Psalm 82:1.
12. Psalm 84:1-2.

has ordained for this work have been given a signet of authority to speak what Jesus speaks, for us to be forgiven, cleansed, and made whole again. These awesome words, "I forgive you," restore us to sweet fellowship with our heavenly Father.

> *"If you forgive anyone's sins, their sins are forgiven;*
> *if you do not forgive them, they are not forgiven."*
> (John 20:23)

Those who serve to minister in our gatherings are given authority to speak forgiveness. But all disciples of Christ are called to confess our sins to each other and forgive. We are all called to release those who have harmed or offended us. It might also be said that misunderstandings, hurt feelings, and offenses will happen where two or three fallible people are gathered together. Forgiving each other clears the air and roots out all bitterness and anger. Forgiveness unites us in a bond of loving fellowship.

One person's sin affects everyone in a worship gathering. It's as if someone comes into our assembly with thistles hitchhiking on his pant legs. The guy who gets too close gets stickers caught on his pants too, and soon everyone is itching and scratching their legs. But there is hope for this thorny problem. The person who is called to minister forgives all who confess their sin. And then, just as we have been forgiven, each one should forgive the person who spread his "thistles" around. When we forgive each other, we get rid of the thorns of sin that grate at us.

Forgiveness brings us peace, heals our wounds, restores our fellowship, and clears the air for true and real worship. The awesome effect of being absolved of our sin is that we come into a reverent awe of the Lord—for He is to be feared.[13] As we receive a pardon for our sin, we learn how to forgive others. This is a vital lesson because we are forgiven in like manner.[14]

Life as a Christian means we walk on a narrow path. It's as if we get up in the morning determined to stick to the right course all day. But then we return home, cut by thistles and thorns because our feet slipped from the path. Each day's missteps are confessed in the evening, and we repent with full assurance of God's mercy.

In our private prayers, we ask Father God to "forgive us our sins," and this opens our hearts to receive His mercy. Once forgiven, our hearts are prepared to forgive and receive the forgiveness proclaimed in the assembly of believers. Our sins, whether secret or known, stain the whole body of Christ

---

13. Psalm 130:4.
14. Matthew 6:14.

and cause all who are called by His holy name to come under the cloud of sin. Because we are one in Christ, it is good for all of us together to be forgiven. In forgiveness the body of Christ is made whole.

To those who lead us, Jesus gave authority to breathe out His words, as if echoing the Father's words, "I forgive you." When we confess our failures, and determine to turn from our wrongdoing, our heavenly Father speaks out words of forgiveness by the breath of the Spirit. Jesus our mediator and High Priest, who serves in heaven's sanctuary, speaks the words spoken by the Father. And by means of the Spirit of Christ, those who minister before us in our gatherings breathe out the same precious words: "I forgive you."

When we obey God's command to forgive each other, we strengthen our bond of fellowship. Prayers lifted up in harmonious agreement are powerful and effective. In an atmosphere of peace and forgiveness, the doors are flung wide open to triumphant, celebrative worship.

> *Therefore I want the men[15] everywhere to pray,*
> *lifting up holy hands without anger or disputing.*
> (1 Timothy 2:8)

Forgiveness in community is vital to the well-being of our gatherings. We ought to enter into our worship assemblies with our hearts prepared to put others' offenses behind us. Before we lift up holy hands to worship, we should forgive each other so we can come together in harmonious song. To keep our ministry and service from being hindered, we should first release people from their wrongs against us and come together in one accord.

This is the power of forgiveness in our worship assemblies, in Jesus' name.

---

15. Used generically, includes both men and women.

21. Forgiveness in Gathering
Q & A

1. Is the sin we commit our problem alone, or does it have a wider impact?

2. Describe the price that was paid for your forgiveness.

3. Who has authority to proclaim God's forgiveness in worship gatherings?

4. What part does confessing to God, repenting and turning from our sin have in forgiveness proclaimed in our assemblies?

My Journal Notes:

Chapter 22
Baptism Unites us with Christ

Key Scriptures:

- "Or don't you know that all of us who were baptized into Christ Jesus were baptized into his death? We were therefore buried with him through baptism into death in order that, just as Christ was raised from the dead through the glory of the Father, we too may live a new life. For if we have been united with him in a death like his, we will certainly also be united with him in a resurrection like his." (Romans 6:3–5)

- "Having been buried with him in baptism, in which you were also raised with him through your faith in the working of God, who raised him from the dead. When you were dead in your sins and in the uncircumcision of your flesh, God made you alive with Christ. He forgave us all our sins, having canceled the charge of our legal indebtedness, which stood against us and condemned us; he has taken it away, nailing it to the cross. And having disarmed the powers and authorities, he made a public spectacle of them, triumphing over them by the cross." (Colossians 2:12–15)

- "Just as a body, though one, has many parts, but all its many parts form one body, so it is with Christ. For we were all baptized by one Spirit so as to form one body—whether Jews or Gentiles, slave or free—and we were all given the one Spirit to drink. Even so the body is not made up of one part but of many. Now if the foot should say, 'Because I am not a hand, I do not belong to the body,' it would not for that reason stop being part of the body." (1 Corinthians 12:12–15)

- "So in Christ Jesus you are all children of God through faith, for all of you who were baptized into Christ have clothed yourselves with Christ. There is neither Jew nor Gentile, neither slave nor free, nor is there male and female, for you are all one in Christ Jesus. If you belong to Christ, then you are Abraham's seed, and heirs according to the promise." (Galatians 3:26–29)

- "Jesus answered, 'Very truly I tell you, no one can enter the kingdom of God unless they are born of water and the Spirit. Flesh gives birth to flesh, but the Spirit gives birth to spirit. You should not be surprised at my saying, "You must be born again." The wind blows wherever it pleases. You hear its sound, but you cannot tell where it comes from or where it is going. So it is with everyone born of the Spirit.'" (John 3:5–8)

Baptism is a life-changing miracle for all who receive the gift of faith in Jesus Christ. The water and the word give witness that the seed of saving faith has come to life in our heart of hearts. This sign is for all who come to believe in our Lord Jesus Christ and His work on the cross. Faith is sufficient, for baptism is a confident hope in Jesus as Lord and Savior who gave His blood to be shed so that we might be forgiven and washed clean of even the stain of sin. Baptism gives witness of our trust in Jesus who gave His body to be broken so that we might be made whole in body, soul, and spirit. The baptized are brought into the church as a part of the whole family to function as part of the body. We are baptized into Christ, His death and His resurrection. Baptism also serves as an adoption rite—another forever kind of miracle.

When we attend a holy baptism, we become an eyewitness to a great wonder. We also serve as a witness to a brother or sister's expression of faith in Christ so we can stand with them in their faith. When we hear a convert's confession of faith in Jesus Christ and understand the powerful effect of the water and the word, it will turn our world upside down. Being a witness to a new creation in Christ, who is made to serve as a part of the body of Christ, is awesome in every way.

Consider the powerful effect of this miracle. When we are baptized into Christ, we are brought into the person of Christ. In the waters of baptism and by the power of the word, we enter into Christ in His death, burial, and resurrection. In baptism, we enter into Christ Jesus who has, by the work of the cross, satisfied all of what God requires. Our baptism immerses us in Christ, saturates us in Christ, and we are made a part of the whole body of Christ which is His church. In Christ, we are rescued from God's righteous wrath, and the Holy Spirit seals and protects us from God's just and righteous judgment against sin.[1]

It doesn't work to say we are in Christ but then separate ourselves from His body.[2] When we detach ourselves, it's like we shrug off the miraculous gift of our baptism. Apart from gathering in Jesus' name, we will soon forget the miracle that baptism accomplished in us. A Christian baptism makes us a new creation, to serve as part of the whole body of Christ, and we do well to joyfully gather and celebrate with others of like faith.

Let's be clear, we are not baptized into a church organization or religious denomination. We are not baptized into the Methodist, Lutheran, Presbyterian, or Catholic church. We are not baptized to be a part of the Vineyard

---

1. 1 Thessalonians 1:10.
2. There are incredible exceptions to this truth. Many times, imprisoned, enslaved, and isolated Christians find abundant comfort in God's holy presence. They are never alone, and they can never be separated from the love of Christ. (Romans 8:35)

Church or Calvary Chapel. No, we are baptized into Christ and His living, active body—the church universal. A church organization may have different customs or rites for baptisms, but they cannot claim the baptized as their exclusive disciples. The baptized are in Christ and made part of His whole body, the church universal. This means that an Anglican Christian in Nigeria and the Pentecostal believer in New York are called to be one in Christ. They are incorporated to function as part of the whole body of Christ.

Baptism is like glue that cements Christians together as one in the Holy Spirit. Baptism in the name of the Father, Son, and Holy Spirit certifies, like having three signatures on our adoption certificate. The water and the word of baptism make us contributing parts of God's family. We are made part of the church and brought into Christ to fulfill our calling and our function as part of His body. Our purpose is to serve as members of the body with the very heart, mind, and attitude of Christ.

The power and significance of baptism is infinite. A whole new life, a new family, a clear worldview, and a community of faith are opened to us. But even more than this, we are baptized into Christ to whom the heavens are open. Now we have the favor of heaven, and the face of God shines upon all of us together in the family of God. In baptism, God Almighty declares us to be His sons and daughters, saying, "This is my beloved." When we are baptized into Christ, we are made to be an integral part in the cause of the kingdom.

Both the one who makes people holy and those who are made holy are of the same family. So Jesus is not ashamed to call them brothers and sisters.
(Hebrews 2:11)

If you think you have never seen a genuine miracle, I would encourage you to witness a baptism. What you will see before your eyes is a beautiful reflection of the ministry of our Lord Jesus Christ. The miracle of baptism takes place in heaven's sanctuary where the High Priest of the church ministers. The water and the word are ministered before your eyes, and the baptized miraculously becomes a brand-new creation in Christ. And then we live in the reality of baptism as we die to ourselves, to be raised up in the power of the resurrected Christ.

This awesome miracle is ministered to cause a new, redeemed soul to become an effective part of the body of Christ in the community of believers. John the Baptizer immersed Jesus in the waters of the Jordan River. After this, Jesus gathered His disciples saying, "Follow me." Phillip baptized the Ethiopian who went back to his home country where he preached the saving faith he had come to know. In faith, as a new creation in Christ, the Ethiopian gathered new believers to his Lord and Savior. On the day of Pentecost in Acts, one hundred and twenty disciples were gathered together to pray. The Spirit of Christ came upon them with power, as tongues of fire. This resulted in over three thousand who came to Christ and were baptized. And then, the church continued to grow in numbers every day.[3]

By the miraculous power of the water and the word, you too can be a part of this great miracle that makes you a new creation in Christ, a son or daughter, a brother or sister in the family of God. The miracle of baptism continues as Christ lives in us day by day.

I have been crucified with Christ and I no longer live, but Christ lives in me. The life I now live in the body, I live by faith in the Son of God, who loved me and gave himself for me.
(Galatians 2:20)

22. Baptism Unites Us with Christ
Q & A

1. Describe the miracle of baptism in the name of the Father, Son, and Holy Spirit.

2. Why is it significant that we are baptized into Christ and not into a church denomination?

3. Is it important for Christians to obey Christ and follow Him in baptism?

4. Describe the reality of baptism as it is lived out in our everyday lives.

---

3. Acts 2:41.

My Journal Notes:

Chapter 23
The Miracle of the Lord's Table

Key Scriptures:

- "And he took bread, and when he had given thanks, he broke it and gave it to them, saying, 'This is my body, which is given for you. Do this in remembrance of me.' And likewise, the cup after they had eaten, saying, 'This cup that is poured out for you is the new covenant in my blood.'" (Luke 22:19–20 ESV)

- "Is not the cup of thanksgiving for which we give thanks a participation in the blood of Christ? And is not the bread that we break a participation in the body of Christ? Because there is one loaf, we, who are many, are one body, for we all share the one loaf." (1 Corinthians 10:16–17)

A house without a table for family to gather around isn't a home. If the tables were removed from a wedding banquet it would be awkward for friends and relatives to gather and share a celebratory meal. Everywhere we go, there's another table. Some houses have little Formica kitchen tables with chrome legs while others have linen-covered dining room tables with silver candlesticks. Parks have picnic tables where mom's potato salad tastes better than ever. Restaurants are filled with the happy noise of people gathered in rooms filled with tables, chairs, and conversation. Offices have long conference tables where business minds come together to make plans. Ambassadors come to a negotiating table to resolve international disputes. But the greatest, most life-changing table is found where God's people gather in Jesus' name.

Rewind a few thousand years to see the tribes of Israel receive the blessings of a holy table where they gathered for their festivals. The people came together on special days to partake of sacrifices in the Lord's presence. David hid out in the wilderness where he sang about the table the Lord set before him in the presence of his enemies. The tables of Israel's rulers offered a welcome respite for those who found favor with the king.

Today, Christians come together in remembrance of Christ to celebrate at a table that overflows with forgiveness and eternal blessing. In this study, we will learn about the abundance set before us. We'll discover how important it is to examine ourselves to know if our hearts seek what has no part in Christ. Because our sinful nature tends to draw us away, we are cautioned not to come to the Lord's Table with divided loyalties. It's important to ask ourselves if we show contempt for the Lord's Table by also partaking at the table of iniquity. In the first segment of this study, we will learn that we must come to partake of Christ with undivided hearts. The oracles of the prophets and apostles will help us see the nature of God—His heart of grace, mercy, and forgiveness.

Then we will learn how the communion table unites all Christians in Christ. This unifying effect is one of the miraculous works of the Lord's Table. When we understand the power of partaking of Christ, in covenant relationship, the strengthening effect of communion will become evident, and our desire to partake of Christ will grow.

This chapter is not intended to be a complete teaching on the communion of the Lord's Table but a study on the risks and abundant benefits of gathering where we are unified as one in Christ.

Think of the simple joy that is ours at many tables that give us as a place to stop, sit down, and offer up a prayer of thanksgiving. This is a respite where we strengthen our physical bodies with delicious and nutritious food. A person's life is often shaped by the interactions around a table. During the holiday seasons, we gather around festive tables to celebrate the occasion. A shared meal nourishes our bodies, and these special moments have the effect of binding us together. That's the benefit of gathering with family and friends around a common table in our homes.

But we have a greater gift in Christ. We are brought to a bountiful table to partake of Christ, and the abundance of His table overflows with blessings. Even when enemies surround us, Jesus prepares an opulent table before us. This is a table that fully satisfies. In a dry and thirsty land, we come to a table of refuge in the presence of God Who Provides.

With a plentiful table set before us, how could we possibly want to take part in any other table? But like the fruit that was pleasing to Eve's eye, the deceptive bounty on the table of malice tempts us to divide our loyalties.

You cannot drink the cup of the Lord and the cup of demons too;
you cannot have a part in both the Lord's Table and the table of demons.
(1 Corinthians 10:21)

These are strong words and must be taken as a serious warning. God jealously guards His children to keep us from anything that would destroy our faith. The Lord shields us from the enemy's fiery darts as He gathers us in His name, and there is no greater protection we can seek. James offers words of warning against divided loyalties:

> *That person should not expect to receive anything from the Lord.*
> *Such a person is double-minded and unstable in all they do.*
> (James 1:7–8)

A divided heart creates a schism between us and our heavenly Father and will tear us from the fellowship of those who gather in Jesus' name. The consequences of contempt for the Lord's Table are serious:

> *That is why many among you are weak and sick,*
> *and a number of you have fallen asleep.*
> (1 Corinthians 11:30)

What does it mean to partake of the cup of evil spirits? This is important to consider because when we determine to continue participating in the cup of evil, it creates a chasm between us and Christ.

> *It is impossible for those who have once been enlightened, who have tasted the heavenly gift, who have shared in the Holy Spirit, who have tasted the goodness of the word of God and the powers of the coming age and who have fallen away, to be brought back to repentance. To their loss they are crucifying the Son of God all over again and subjecting him to public disgrace.*
> (Hebrews 6:4–6)

When we gather at the Lord's Table, claim the name of Christ as our own, and then also partake at the table of evil, we find ourselves caught in major conflict.

> *May the table set before them become a snare; may it become retribution and a trap.*
> *May their eyes be darkened so they cannot see, and their backs be bent forever.*
> (Psalm 69:22–23)

When our hearts are divided between what is holy and what exalts our sinful nature, we show scorn and contempt for the Bread and the Cup. Our hearts are torn in two when we eat the Bread of Life and the bread of injustice. The heavens become like brass to the prayers of those who show such contempt. We are separated from the comfort, the intercessions, and the joys of fellowship in Jesus' name.

> *"No one can serve two masters. Either you will hate the one and love the other, or you will be devoted to the one and despise the other. You cannot serve both God and money."*
> (Matthew 6:24)

The truth is, the work of anxious labor can never satisfy. In fact, when we seek to satisfy our sinful nature at the table of desire, we are left with a hunger for more of the same.

> *You will eat but not be satisfied; your stomach will still be empty.*
> (Micah 6:14)

This Proverb describes the appetites of those with divided hearts:

> *They eat the bread of wickedness and drink the wine of violence.*
> (Proverbs 4:17)

Partakers of the bread and cup are brought together, but participation in the Lord's Table and the table of the Evil One rips us apart. We deceive ourselves if we come before the Lord with a rebellious heart. If we continue to refuse repentance, our stubbornness will defeat us as followers of Christ. This is a part of what it means to come to the table in an unworthy manner, and the consequences are devastating. When we come to the table of communion with a divided heart, we cause Jesus' holy name to be disgraced. If we have one foot in the kingdom of light and the other in the realm of darkness, we must repent of our duplicity before we come to the Lord's Table.

As we come to this gathering, we ought to examine ourselves to see where we stand. Can we serve both God and love the things money can buy? What are we holding back from Christ? Have we committed every part of who we are to Christ? Have we confessed and repented of the sin and confessed our need of Christ?

Because of the serious nature of the Apostle Paul's warnings, it is crucial to pray for God's grace and mercy upon those who come to partake of the bread and the cup but may not have fully examined themselves. Some may come who are caught in sin's grip and want to be set free. The Bible offers a picture of the Lord's abundant mercies from King Hezekiah's day:

> *Although most of the many people who came from Ephraim, Manasseh, Issachar and Zebulun had not purified themselves, yet they ate the Passover, contrary to what was written. But Hezekiah prayed for them, saying, "May the Lord, who is good, pardon everyone who sets their heart on seeking God–the Lord, the God of their ancestors–even if they are not clean according to the rules of the sanctuary."*
> *And the Lord heard Hezekiah and healed the people.*
> (2 Chronicles 30:18–20)

Prayers for mercy and healing are vital because the heart of God is toward mercy. Mercy always trumps judgment in the kingdom of heaven. Now, with ample words of caution, and the promise of God's boundless forgiveness and mercy, let's move forward to the blessings of the Lord's Table.

In ancient times, an invitation to dine at a king's table meant you were brought into his realm of provision and protection. King David offered the shelter of his table to the son of Jonathan, his covenant companion.

So Mephibosheth ate at David's table like one of the king's sons.
(2 Samuel 9:11)

Because David had cut a covenant with Jonathan, he offered Mephibosheth the comfort of gathering around the king's table. In the same way, we are strengthened together in a bond with Christ as we come together at the table of our covenant.

Bible history teaches us that participation in Christ by means of the bread and cup of communion is powerful and effective. Real life stories illustrating this truth are offered as examples throughout the Scriptures. When Abraham returned victorious over his enemies, Melchizedek set a table before him with bread and wine. Moses gave us a preview of this rite of the church with the table of the Presence in the tabernacle. On the way to the cross, Jesus instituted this supper of blessing and forgiveness, commanding all disciples, present and future, to: "Do this in remembrance of me." Still today, we are called to come into God's holy presence, in Christ, for a celebration of remembrance at the Lord's Table. His presence is abundantly evident each time we come together around the table. This is a heaven-sent gathering where our Lord and Savior is present with us. It's an assembly ordained in the Kingdom of Heaven.

When we gather to commune, we reach out to receive the bread and the cup as individuals and partake of Christ's body and blood to be strengthened together as one in Him. As partakers of the elements of communion, we give witness that we are joined together with Christ in His death. With two hands, we reach out to receive the benefits of the cross, and then, as we partake of the bread and cup, we are bound together, and many hands are joined as one in Jesus' name.

When we eat the bread of communion and drink from the cup of the Lord's Table, we affirm that we are joined together in Christ, united with Him and His body, the Church. We acknowledge that we stand together in faith with our fellow communicants at the Lord's Table. When Christians receive the cup of the Lord's Table, we become partakers in the blood Jesus poured out for the remission of our sins. As we receive the bread of the Lord's supper, we reaffirm that we are members of His body, in communion with Christ. Jesus' body was broken, and for those who are in Christ our flesh is also broken so that we may be made part of the whole body of Christ.

When we partake together in the bounty of communion, it is a united proclamation: "We are called by Jesus' holy name. We are members of Christ,

His death, His suffering, and His resurrection. We are beckoned to come, to enter into His love and to receive forgiveness and mercy. We are united with our brothers and sisters in forgiveness." Indeed, we are brought together in His mercy, and the whole assembly is forgiven. God's children are brought together in the love of Christ, and His love continues with us just as the bread of the Presence always remained in the Old Testament temple.

It's a reality that every denomination has prescribed traditions and practices for gathering at the Lord's Table, but they are external differences. For some, the Lord's Table is an ordinance, and for others, a sacrament. But there is no separation when we commune in Christ. There are neither Jew nor Greek, slave nor free, neither rich nor poor, male nor female, weak nor powerful at the table of communion. Methodists, Episcopalians, Pentecostals, Baptists, Catholics, and Lutherans, who are in Christ, are all as one at the Lord's Table. The barriers are broken down for all who receive the bread and the cup of the Lord in His presence. Nationalities can't divide us because we are joined together with Christians in every tribe, nation, people, and culture. All religious labels are torn away and as we partake of Christ, we are united in Christ as one body. In his letter to the Corinthian church, the Apostle Paul asked a pertinent question:

Is Christ divided?
(1 Corinthians 1:13)

Then, he admonished them for their divisiveness, and taught them there is only one Lord and Savior. In the light of Christ, labels fall away, and walls are torn down. In the knowledge of Christ, we step up to the Lord's Table where our hearts are united. In His holy presence is healing to make us whole as one—the body of Christ.

In this study we have come to see the need to examine ourselves, repent and receive God's mercy and forgiveness. We entered into the joy of the Lord as we hold out our hands with expectation to receive and partake of the bread and cup of our covenant with Christ. Now we know about the great comfort of participation in Christ at the communion table that unites us as one body. We have become aware of our Savior who is actively present and who remains with us, uniting us with people of every nation and language. Indeed, we are all made one in Christ.

In the light of this truth, how is it possible for Christians to desire anything that distracts from the bounty of the Lord's Table? This study of God's Word has led us to know the dangers of partaking of the Bread of Life and also the bread of injustice. Our hearts are brought to repent of our duplicity.

The consequences for divided hearts are too devastating to ignore. We come to the Lord's Table with contrite hearts to receive His forgiveness and mercy.

The holy Scriptures in this chapter have shown us the incredible joy that is ours when we partake of Christ in the bread and the cup of communion. When we taste of the Lord's goodness in the bounty set before us, all Christians are joined together as one in our Lord Jesus. At the Lord's Table, we reaffirm our covenant with Christ as we eat the bread and drink from the cup. Together we are strengthened as one in the Lord. With this knowledge, we are compelled to partake of Christ, of His body that was broken and His blood that was shed, and to commune often until He comes again.

The power and effect of the Lord's Table is both immediate and eternal. The blood of the Lamb cleanses us from even the stain of sin. We are forgiven and thereby protected from God's holy and righteous wrath. In Jesus' broken body there is healing. The Bread of Life strengthens us in soul and spirit. As we gather to partake of Christ, the bread and the cup of the Lord's Table, we are fortified in our union with Christ and His body, the Church.

Jesus still breaks the bread and says to today's disciples, "This is my body given for you; do this in remembrance of me." He takes up the cup of His covenant in this hour, saying, "This cup is the new covenant in my blood, which is poured out for you."

23. The Miracle of the Lord's Table
Q & A

1. Describe the abundance, the fragrance, and the joy of gathering before the Lord's Table.

2. How does partaking of the bread and cup of the Lord's Table bring God's people into unity?

3. Why is it important to take part of the Lord's Table and no other table?

4. What declaration do we make by standing with our brothers and sisters to partake of Christ at the communion table?

5. Why is it important to examine ourselves before gathering to partake of Christ around the Lord's Table?

My Journal Notes:

Chapter 24
Gathered to God's People

Key Scriptures:

- "Then Abraham breathed his last and died at a good old age, an old man and full of years; and he was gathered to his people." (Genesis 25:8)

- "Concerning the coming of our Lord Jesus Christ and our being gathered to him, we ask you, brothers and sisters, not to become easily unsettled or alarmed." (2 Thessalonians 2:1–2)

- "For the Lord himself will come down from heaven, with a loud command, with the voice of the archangel and with the trumpet call of God, and the dead in Christ will rise first." (1 Thessalonians 4:16)

The Apostle Paul wrote to the Christians in Thessalonica to comfort them with knowledge of what happens after we "fall asleep" in death. He offered hope in the resurrected Christ. His words strengthened their faith, assuring them that those who sleep in death will precede those who remain until the trumpet call of God sounds to call us home. When the archangel sounds the ram's horn, the "dead in Christ will rise first."[1]

This great assurance of God's power and might to save, and to carry us across that great threshold into His glory, is the focus of this study. May our faith be strengthened to know that we will be raised up to dwell with the Lord God forever.

At the end of life here on planet earth, we will be brought across a vast threshold into life forever in the presence of our Lord God. When our earthly tent is folded up, and our stakes pulled up from terra firma, we will be gathered to those who have gone before us. We know this is true because many years after Abraham departed from this earth, God spoke to Moses, saying:

> "I am the God of your father, the God of Abraham,
> the God of Isaac and the God of Jacob."
> (Exodus 3:6)

God spoke to Moses in his day and time and referred to Abraham in the present. We have God's spoken word as proof that when we sleep in death, we will be present with the Lord.[2] We have His written promise. How can there be any room for doubt?

---

1. 1 Thessalonians 4:16.
2. 2 Corinthians 5:8.

An awesome example of this truth occurred on the Mount of Transfiguration.[3] Moses and Elijah appeared with Jesus even though Moses had died and was buried on Mount Nebo in Moab many years before. Elijah was taken up to heaven in a whirlwind hundreds of years before this, and he remained to appear with Jesus the Messiah at His transfiguration.

Jesus faced down the hyper-religious Sadducees who came to Him with trick questions. They attempted to justify their unbelief in God's resurrection power and tried to trap Jesus with His own words. But He told them that they were wrong because they didn't believe God's word and denied the power of God. Jesus' answer gives us a blessed hope of resurrection after we are gathered together with those who have gone before us.

Jesus replied, "You are in error because you do not know the Scriptures or the power of God. At the resurrection people will neither marry nor be given in marriage; they will be like the angels in heaven. But about the resurrection of the dead–have you not read what God said to you, 'I am the God of Abraham, the God of Isaac, and the God of Jacob'? He is not the God of the dead but of the living."
(Matthew 22:29–32)

Jesus taught them this beautiful and awesome truth about resurrection power. Because we believe what Jesus' taught, after our last day on earth we can still say, "the Lord is my Shepherd." He shepherds us as we pass from this life after our last gasp for breath. The Good Shepherd leads us to dwell in His house forever. He escorts us over the threshold and through the gates and into the city of our God. His reward is with Him, and each of us will receive our eternal reward.

The Lord Almighty showed His might and strength as He brought the tribes of Israel out of Egypt with a show of His sovereign power. He divided the great waters of the Red Sea. The people crossed over on dry ground. God delivered His people and destroyed the oppressors who pursued them.

So the Lord brought us out of Egypt with a mighty hand and an outstretched arm, with great terror and with signs and wonders.
(Deuteronomy 26:8)

With the same might and power, the Great El Shaddai takes us over the great divide, into the presence of all those who have gone before us. Is our Lord and God able to deliver us from the grip of this world? Oh, yes! He is more than able. He is faithful to accomplish all that He has purposed and planned. The Almighty will fulfill every promise in the book. Listen to the words of the psalmist as he sings out with words of God's deliverance:

---
3. Matthew 17.

When Israel came out of Egypt, Jacob from a people of foreign tongue,
Judah became God's sanctuary, Israel his dominion.

The sea looked and fled, the Jordan turned back;
the mountains leaped like rams, the hills like lambs.

Why was it, sea, that you fled? Why, Jordan, did you turn back?
Why, mountains, did you leap like rams, you hills, like lambs?

Tremble, earth, at the presence of the Lord,
at the presence of the God of Jacob,
who turned the rock into a pool, the hard rock into springs of water.
(Psalm 114)

Those who fear the Lord have no need to fear the grave because it holds no power over them. All people are destined to die once, and yet we know beyond any doubt that all those who are in Christ, by faith, will stand before our righteous and just Judge covered in Jesus' robe of righteousness.

In the sleep of death our soul and spirit separate from the body. Our mortal body perishes, but spirit and soul are imperishable and return to the One who breathed life into us. The Father sends his holy angels to carry our soul and spirit upward. The angels are ministering spirits to all those whose names are written in the Book of Life. These heavenly beings minister to God's people while we live upon the earth, and they continue to watch over us after we have breathed our last breath. The eternal part of a person is not bound to earth but goes to be in the presence of Christ. When we pass from this life, the separation of body from soul and spirit is a great leap upward.

It's as if a celebrative parade occurs in the heavens when God calls us home. Not only one angel comes to accompany us into God's holy presence but many. It's a victorious procession to the garden of our God. We are lifted up by a royal throng of angels to guard our way through unknown domains filled with peril, to take us into the embrace of those who have gone before us. This procession of honor is for all who are victorious in Christ, who overcome by the blood of the Lamb of God. We are brought to the cloud of witnesses, heroes of our faith, as if joining them in the grandstands to cheer on those who will follow.

God's ministering angels greet us at the moment of our passing. They bid us welcome and revive us from the cares, sorrows, and tears of the life we have left behind. God's angels usher us into Jesus' loving arms, the Good Shepherd of the sheep, where He has prepared a bountiful feast for us. We will join the Apostle "whom Jesus loved"[4] to lean on Jesus' breast in joyful celebration.

---
4. John 13:23.

A great old hymn written by Robert Lowry sings of a river from the throne of God that washes us in its precious tide.

> Shall we gather at the river,
> Where bright angel feet have trod,
> With its crystal tide forever
> Flowing by the throne of God?
>
> Yes, we'll gather at the river,
> The beautiful, the beautiful river;
> Gather with the saints at the river
> That flows by the throne of God.
>
> On the margin of the river,
> Washing up its silver spray,
> We will talk and worship ever,
> All the happy golden day.
>
> Ere we reach the shining river,
> Lay we every burden down;
> Grace our spirits will deliver,
> And provide a robe and crown.
>
> At the smiling of the river,
> Mirror of the Savior's face,
> Saints, whom death will never sever,
> Lift their songs of saving grace.
>
> Soon we'll reach the silver river,
> Soon our pilgrimage will cease;
> Soon our happy hearts will quiver
> With the melody of peace.[5]

We leave a legacy of faith and godliness for those who follow in our footsteps. Grandchildren receive a blessing from grandparents who leave an inheritance for them.[6] Aunts and uncles build a legacy with stories that reveal family values. But whether we are rich or beggar, a king on a royal throne or vagrant who sits in the dust, we are gathered together as one in the presence of the Lord. The treasures we left on earth will become moth-eaten. The material things we treasured during our lives may be stolen and just corrode away. But what we have stored up in heaven is kept safe, an eternal treasure waiting for us.

---

5. Robert Lowry, composer, "Shall We Gather at the River?", Happy Voices, 1865.
6. Proverbs 13:22.

We are instructed to not give up gathering together with our brothers and sisters in Christ to worship, serve, and minister before the Lord. The purpose for assembling together is clear: Fellowship in His name benefits each of us for eternity.

And let us consider how we may spur one another on toward love and good deeds, not giving up meeting together, as some are in the habit of doing, but encouraging one another–and all the more as you see the Day approaching.
(Hebrews 10:24–25)

As we gather together to worship with the saints during the days of our lives here on earth, we get a whiff of the pleasing fragrance of Christ when we will be gathered to Him at the trumpet sound. We will be gathered with all the saints who have gone before us and will be raised up in resurrection power to enter the joy of the Lord forever and ever.

Maranatha![7]

---

7. Maranatha means "come, our Lord!" in Aramaic.

24. Gathered to God's People
Q & A

1. How do we know that when we sleep in death, we will be gathered to those who have gone before us?

2. What examples from the Bible are given to assure us of God's resurrection power?

3. What does it mean that the grave has no power over God's people?

4. How does gathering together in Jesus' name prepare us to be gathered together with the heroes of our faith who have gone before us?

My Journal Notes:

Chapter 25
We Assemble to Prepare for the Great Gathering

Key Scriptures:

- "You turned to God from idols to serve the living and true God, and to wait for his Son from heaven, whom he raised from the dead, Jesus who delivers us from the wrath to come." (1 Thessalonians 1:10 ESV)

- "When he comes on that day, he will receive glory from his holy people—praise from all who believe. And this includes you, for you believed what we told you about him." (2 Thessalonians 1:10 NLT)

- "Let us rejoice and be glad and give him glory! For the wedding of the Lamb has come, and his bride has made herself ready. Fine linen, bright and clean, was given her to wear." (Revelation 19:7-8)

The world around us seems to wax and wane politically and spiritually. People's biases and convictions swing back and forth like a pendulum. Fashions change for every season. Human nature leads us to focus on the far left and far right swing, where the bob seems to stop for a split second. But in fact, this is only a flash in the momentum. It's too easy to forget what is in between. The Apostle Paul warned against limiting our view to the onethe to one end of the spectrum.

If only for this life we have hope in Christ,
we are of all people most to be pitied.
(1 Corinthians 15:19)

Some followers of Christ only see the far end of the swing, thinking that what we do in this life doesn't matter all that much, we just need Jesus to get us into heaven where all our troubles will finally be over. Extreme views of life and eternity are the farthest swings of the pendulum's bob. As an example, we are predisposed to hear the first and last words of a speech but have to take notes to remember the main part. As Christians, our tendency is to focus too much on the present or limit our attention to an eternal glory. Some of us tend to excuse our present troubles with a sigh in favor of the grandeur we will be part of in heaven. An old-time preacher described this view as, "Pie in the sky in the sweet bye and bye." The other extreme is when we make it our cause to fix the world by our own efforts to establish God's eternal kingdom now so we can rescue this present world from its decay.

In reality, these are the farthest swings of the pendulum and become extreme if we use either end to limit our viewpoint and mission. The truth is that we do have a great hope of God's eternal glory, and we are offered a taste of heaven right now. It's not like eternity is something that will happen only in the future—eternity is now and forever. Jesus is preparing a place for us to dwell in the Father's house forevermore.[1] Until then we are sojourners on the earth and seek to know His presence as we come into His house of prayer. In our fellowship and worship gatherings today it's as if we get a Costco size sample of heaven, but we get to enjoy the whole enchilada after we check out and go home. How and where do we get this taste of heaven that prepares us, as a bride, for the coming Yeshua HaMashiach?[2] The focus of this study is on the present-day blessings of gathering together in Jesus' name that prepare us as the bride of Christ—adorned in the present, living in His presence every day of our lives, and then glorified in eternity. Take time to stop and meditate on each of the citations below. In your study groups, take the time to look up the Scripture footnotes and discuss each segment. And may your cup overflow with God's blessings.

There are many ways to taste and see that the Lord is good;[3] and His goodness is both now and forever. When our eyes are opened to see God's eternal glory, His joy puts a dance in our stride as we take the step of faith into God's eternal glory.

Today is the day to come, by faith, into covenant with Christ, obey His command to "believe and be baptized," and then our hearts look forward to hearing His precious words: "Come, you who are blessed by my Father; take your inheritance, the kingdom prepared for you since the creation of the world."[4]

A morning quiet time for prayer and worship makes our morning better and prepares us for worship with the angels in glory forever. Our hearts leap for joy with the rising of the sun because He is our strength and shield, our ever-present help in times of trouble, and we look forward to the day our sorrow and tears will be wiped away forevermore. Our Lord and God satisfies us in the morning with His unfailing love, so that we may sing for joy and be forever glad.[5]

We gather together in triumphant worship, shout for joy, and lift up our banners in Jesus' name, knowing our Lord will stand victorious upon the earth with all things under His feet.[6]

---

1. John 14:3.
2. The Anointed One.
3. Psalm 34:8.
4. Matthew 25:34.
5. Psalm 90:14.
6. Psalm 20:5.

With joy and delight we come to worship before God's altar to prepare us to exalt the Father before His throne in heaven.[7]

We sing and make music to the Lord in our worship gatherings, and we will worship with ten-thousand voices of angels before the throne of God forever and ever.[8]

In God's holy presence our mourning is turned to dancing in this present day, and we are clothed with an eternal joy.[9]

We sing Jesus' new song, playing our instruments with skill, so our hearts can savor God's promise of eternal goodness and glory.[10]

The earth is filled with awe as evening fades into the sounds of joyful song because of all God has done on our behalf. As the dusk fades to darkness of night, songs of thanksgiving prepare our hearts for the day when there will be no more night, and no darkness.[11]

Shouts of joy surround us in our gatherings of praise, knowing we will soon hear the sound of trumpets to call us home evermore.[12]

The Lord of Glory primes us with the joy of His presence, so we may "enter into the joy of the Lord"[13] forever.

God gave us a Sabbath rest to enter in our day, and as we put aside the cares of this world, we get a taste of God's eternal rest. This rest was established on the seventh day of creation, and in it is the eternal light of life that drives out the darkness and chaos of this world.[14]

Obeying our Lord's commands brings joy and strength to our hearts in the present and stores up an eternal reward according to our deeds.[15]

Every Christian has a work set apart for them to accomplish in this lifetime,[16] and all who are faithful in the use of talents for the service of the kingdom are prepared for greater responsibilities in glory.[17]

God's people gather together in Jesus' name to worship, and with confidence draw near to the throne of grace to receive mercy and find grace to help them in their time of need,[18] so that they may enter into His mercies on

---

7. Psalm 99:9.
8. Revelation 5:11.
9. Psalm 30:11–12.
10. Psalm 33:3.
11. Revelation 22:5.
12. 1 Thessalonians 4:16.
13. Matthew 25:21.
14. Matthew 11:28.
15. Romans 2:6.
16. Ephesians 2:10.
17. Matthew 25:14–30.
18. Hebrews 4:16.

the day of the Lord.

Jesus' followers come together to speak and hear the oracles of God, faithfully administering His grace, and to ready their hearts to enter into His glory and majesty for ever and ever.[19]

The Good Shepherd sets a table before us in the presence of our enemies to make us ready to dwell in the house of the Lord forever.[20]

Our souls join in a festive throng to ascend to the house of God. Under the shadow of his wings, and with shouts of joy and praise, we celebrate the Lord's everlasting victory.[21]

In joy and gladness, we gather to worship, lifted up to the mountain of the Lord, prepared as a bride to enter the eternal glory of our Lord and King.[22]

The Lord Almighty exalts His people above the enemies who surround us, as He makes us forever victorious over sin and death.[23]

Our Lord Jesus wraps us in His robe of righteousness to prepare us for the day we will see Him robed in splendor, greatness, and strength.[24]

We wait with great expectation, our lamps filled with oil through the night hours. Our eyes look to see our Bridegroom come in His glory to take us to His great wedding feast.[25]

The wonders of the Lord delight us today and offer a glimpse of the beauty and loftiness of the heights of Mount Zion, the eternal city of the Great King.[26]

We come to know the joy of our salvation in the present, and this delight sustains as we prepare to enter the never-ending joy of the Lord.[27]

Jesus throws down the strongholds that stand against those who gather in His name, for He is mighty to save. He makes straight a way for us to see Him face to face, robed in splendor, striding forth in greatness of His eternal strength.[28]

God's people rejoice in sufferings that complete, in our body, "what is still lacking in regard to Christ's afflictions"[29] for the "glory in the church, and in Christ Jesus to all generations forever and ever. Amen."[30]

---

19. 1Peter 4:11.
20. Psalm 23:6.
21. Psalm 42:4.
22. Psalm 45:15.
23. 1 Corinthians 15:55–57.
24. Isaiah 61;10.
25. Matthew 25:6.
26. Psalm 48:2.
27. Psalm 51:12.
28. Isaiah 63:1.
29. Colossians 1:24.
30. Ephesians 3:21.

Rivers that stream through the earth, from the great Amazon to the mighty Nile, the vast Mississippi, and the powerful waves of the Yangtze river all clap their hands as the waters rush down from the mountains to the sea, as if to proclaim the wonders of the eternal river that flows from the throne of God.[31]

Christians are called to be overcomers in Christ, and in Him we rise above all the trouble, trials, worries and temptations of this present world. All who are victorious are given the right to eat from the tree of life.[32] A portion of the hidden manna will be given to all who rise above the cares of this world to enter God's eternal kingdom.

A white stone of absolution[33] and a new name will be granted to those who turn from sin and come with repentant hearts. The victors will be given authority over the nations. Dressed in white, we will come before the Lord, knowing our names are secure in the Book of Life. The overcomers will be pillars in the temple of our God. As conquerors in Christ we will sit with Him on His throne.

We are called to live in the fullness of Christ from the rising of the sun to the setting. Through the watches of the night our thoughts are drawn to the Lord.[34] We stand on the earth and look up to see God's faithful witnesses in the sky, and look forward to the city where the glory of God gives it light, and the Lamb is its lamp.[35]

> *I saw heaven standing open and there before me was a white horse, whose rider is called Faithful and True. With justice he judges and wages war. His eyes are like blazing fire, and on his head are many crowns. He has a name written on him that no one knows but he himself. He is dressed in a robe dipped in blood, and his name is the Word of God. The armies of heaven were following him, riding on white horses and dressed in fine linen, white and clean. Coming out of his mouth is a sharp sword with which to strike down the nations. "He will rule them with an iron scepter." He treads the winepress of the fury of the wrath of God Almighty. On his robe and on his thigh he has this name written:* KING OF KINGS AND LORD OF LORDS.
> (Revelation 19:11–16)

Our Lord Jesus is preparing a bride for Himself. Jesus Christ our High Priest gathers us together in His name to worship, serve, and minister in His presence to make us ready for His coming. Together, in His name, we are adorned with fine linen, precious jewels, bracelets for our wrists, earrings of

---

31. Psalm 98:8, Revelation 22:1.
32. Revelation 2:7.
33. Revelation 2:17.
34. Psalm 63:6.
35. Revelation 21:23.

gold studded with silver, a string of jewels as an ornament for our neck, and a crown for our heads. Together—in community—today, the bride is beautified with the oil of myrrh to prepare for the Bridegroom's great wedding feast.[36] God's people seek to dwell together in the house of the Lord every day of their lives. We long to gaze on the beauty of the Lord and seek Him as we gather to worship,[37] so that we may be readied to dwell with Him forever.

We are called to be faithful in our day and time. His name is to be proclaimed in all the earth as He makes way for the great victory of His justice. All those who stand in opposition to His reign, the kings of the earth and their armies who gathered to make war against Him, will be thrown down. His name is Faithful and True. The mystery of His name is revealed to those who will see. His name is the Word of God, and on His robe and thigh is written the name: king of kings and lord of lords. This is the name that is above all names, and all His enemies will be trampled under His feet because of the power of His name.

> *Blow the trumpet in Zion,*
> *declare a holy fast, call a sacred assembly. Gather the people,*
> *consecrate the assembly; bring together the elders,*
> *gather the children, those nursing at the breast.*
> *Let the bridegroom leave his room and the bride her chamber.*
> (Joel 2:15–16)

---

36. Ezekiel 16:10–13.
37. Psalm 27:4.

25. We Assemble to Prepare for the Great Gathering
Q & A

1. Describe the extreme views of life and eternity that we see at the farthest swings of the pendulum.

2. Which of the citations in this study is most helpful to you as you prepare for the Great Gathering?

3. Why is it important for the bride of Christ to prepare herself for the great wedding banquet?

4. Explain the adornments of the bride of Christ.

My Journal Notes:

Come, Let us Gather

It's amazing that one, short, concise imperative of Scripture that instructs us to "not giving up meeting together"[1] reveals volumes of vital truths to light our pathway. It's like peeling back rose petals to see the flower burst out with fragrance, brilliant colors, and dazzling beauty.

This one little phrase in a verse is like shining light on a diamond to see it refract hundreds of facets of light and sparkle up a whole room. As incredible as it is, when we meditate on the truths of Scripture, the Holy Spirit opens our eyes to see light and truth, and then the Spirit leads us to other verses that test or prove what we are learning. Before long we have a tightly woven fabric of truth—knit together with threads like fine linen, silver, and gold.

A trek through Scripture is an adventurous journey; an impossible journey that is made possible because we serve God whose nature is to reveal Himself to all those who search for Him as if searching for lost valuables.[2]

From the "Great Departure" to the final "Great Gathering," we have learned the value, the blessings and the joys of coming together in Jesus name to be blessed in the ministries of our High Priest, where we minister, serve, and worship before Him.

Together we will come face to face with the King of Kings and Lord of Lords.

---

1. Hebrews 10:25.
2. Luke 15:8–10.

Acknowledgments

Beginning with an eye-opening revelation, and through years of searching to know the heart of God regarding the church, the journey that brought me to write this study book has been filled with friends, teachers, pastors, and fellow learners who have stood with me. My wife, Susie, has supported me with her prayers through many days of early morning research and writing sessions. My editor and friend, Jeff Kincaid, has helped me keep the message clear and concise. My friend Mark Philpot has helped to illuminate the depth and meaning of ancient Hebrew words used for the study of Scriptures.

I'm especially thankful for my family. My grandchildren inspire me to build a godly legacy for them. My sons encourage me with love and support, each in their own special way.

During the final editing and rewriting for *Great Gatherings* a family medical emergency called us away to Southern California. It's ironic that while there, a world-wide pandemic occurred, and all public assemblies were banned. Many churches cancelled on-site gatherings and held virtual services instead.

May this study encourage us to come together again to worship, serve, and minister before the Lord in our worship gatherings.

My most loyal readers are those who came every week to our home Bible study group. I thank every one of them for their prayers and encouragement. Most of all, I thank my dear, departed friend, Ruth Oesteman, for bringing us all together in her home so we could dig into God's word.

www.ingramcontent.com/pod-product-compliance
Lightning Source LLC
Chambersburg PA
CBHW030052100526
44591CB00008B/111